GLASS & CERAMIC
BASKETS

IDENTIFICATION AND VALUE GUIDE

**Carole Bess White
and L. M. White**

COLLECTOR BOOKS
A Division of Schroeder Publishing Co., Inc.

Front cover, from left: Green with gold enameling, 15", attributed to Bohemia, $450.00 – 550.00; blue with thorn handle, 8½", circa 1894 – 1896, $300.00 – 350.00; chintz, Royal Winton, sunshine pattern, 5", marked "Made in England," $100.00 – 135.00.

Cover design: Beth Summers
Book design: Melissa J. Reed

COLLECTOR BOOKS
P.O. Box 3009
Paducah, Kentucky 42002-3009
www.collectorbooks.com

Copyright © 2002 by Carole Bess White & L.M. White

The current values in this book should be used only as a guide. They are not intended to set prices, which vary from one section of the country to another. Auction prices as well as dealer prices vary greatly and are affected by condition as well as demand. Neither the authors nor the publisher assumes responsibility for any losses that might be incurred as a result of consulting this guide.

Searching For A Publisher?

We are always looking for people knowledgeable within their fields. If you feel that there is a real need for a book on your collectible subject and have a large comprehensive collection, contact Collector Books.

Contents

Dedication & Acknowledgments 4

Introduction: The Basket Case 5

American Glass Baskets .7

Imported Glass Baskets 97

Miscellaneous Glass Baskets 112

Victorian & Early 20th Century Art Glass Baskets .121

American Ceramic Baskets 128

Imported Ceramic Baskets 143

Miscellaneous Ceramic Baskets 181

What Is Dolly Varden? 184

Glass Basket Advertisements 186

Bibliography 198

About the Authors 199

Dedication

This book is dedicated to Ruth McCue, the lady with 1,000+ baskets.

Acknowledgments

Thanks and appreciation to the many collectors who kindly allowed their wonderful baskets to be photographed or who generously shared their knowledge; without their help, this book would not have been possible. Any errors are solely the responsibility of the authors.

Thanks to all the wonderful collectors who let us photograph their collections and advised us:

Philip & Laura Allhand, Allhands Antiques

Nancy, Bill, John & Elizabeth Brewer

Shirley Bolman

Darlene & Gordon Cochran, D & G Antiques

Tim & Robin Cook

Lorraine Duncan

Dorothy Golik

Jewell Gowan, Jewell Collector Reference Books, jewellbook@aol.com

Marv & Trace Faughender

Dennis & Eva Headrick

Ruth McCue

Ron & Donna Miller, publishers of *Old Stuff* newspaper

Linda Steward

Orville & Elsa Trover, Trover's Antiques

Janice Wallace

Thanks to all who helped us, advised us, and identified baskets:

Al & Carol Carder, Carder Country Antiques

Rogene & John Clements

Randy & Debbie Coe, Coe's Mercantile

JoAnn Griffin, www.mccoyandmore.com

Karen McIntyre

Lee & Carol Marple

Lorraine Kovar

Bea & Terry Martin

Dean Six

Neal Skibinski

W. Joanne Voeller

Dennis Warden, Fabupots@aol.com

Speakers and attendees at the American Glass Rally, May 2001

Dealers at the Portland Rain of Glass Show, January 2001 — We shot the show!

Ad Lib Antiques & Collectibles, Bertina Cox

Angel Antiques, Nancy Wilcox

Antiques of Yesteryear, Maxine & Louie Cozzetto

Baker/Richardson Antiques, Fran Baker & Vic Richardson

Bitterroot Antiques, Rebecca Franklin

Carolyn's Antiques, Carolyn Crow

CJ's Glass, John, Cindy, Kristi & Kasandra Frank

Closet Classics, Victor & Dianne Elliott

Cole's Antiques, Richard & Clara Cole

Country Collectibles, Janice Ahl

D&B Enterprises, Dave & Barbara Ownbey

Decorator Antiques, Mark Howard

Dream of Jeanie's, Jean Snook & Norine Millay

Glass & Stuff, Karl & Deborah deJong

Granny Annie's Antiques, Patricia Ann Christiansen

Hodge Podge Antiques, Art & Joyce Biscoe

Hooked on Antiques, Arnie Masoner

J&J Glass, Jim & Jean Campbell

Jay & Nadine Downham, Depression Anxiety

Kathy's Korner, Kathy & Bill Eytcheson

Barbara Kennedy

L&M Glassware, Michael & Leegh Wyse

L&T Collectibles, Lana & Ted Renner

Larsson's Legacy, Swede & Kay Larsson

McCartney's Antiques, Ann & Bob McCartney

My Shop, Dennis Canavan

Nine Lives Antiques, Bill Harmon

Olde Favorites, Marilyn Brodie

Oregon Trail Antiques, Jim & Carletta Roecker

The Owl's Nest Antiques, Evie & Bill Hall

Rose Garden Antiques, Wanda & Bill Rice & Vicky Compston

Royal Antiques & Vancouver Appraisal, Robert & Laurinda Piekow

The Sampler Antiques, Tara Adair & Liz Porter

Thompson's Treasures, Francis & Gretchen Thompson

Timeless Antiques/Deb's Oldies but Goodies, Barbara Johnson

TK Enterprises, Tom & Karin Sanders

Wagon Wheel Antiques, William & Doris Howard

Whistle Stop Antiques, Pat & Forest Bither

To order autographed copies of this book, or for questions and/or discussion, e-mail cbessw@aol.com.

Introduction: The Basket Case

What kind of baskets do you like? Glass? Ceramic? Old? New? Large? Small? Well, you're in luck because there are literally thousands of baskets available in every shape, size, and material imaginable — many, many more than would fit in one volume.

What we've tried to do is narrow down the field to show the most representative glass and ceramic baskets on the market today. This includes older and newer, American-made and foreign-made.

"Big Cookie." Depression-era jade green glass basket with metal handle, Fenton Art Glass Company, 1930s, $275.00 – 350.00.

What exactly is a basket? For the purposes of this book, we will define the basket as a container with a handle made of the same material as the body. True, this rules out a lot of mixed media baskets, such as those pictured in this introduction, but we have to start somewhere!

How are baskets measured? It seems every manufacturer had a different method of measuring the size of their baskets. The A.H. Heisey Company measured theirs from rim to rim. The Duncan Company measured theirs from base to rim. The Roseville Pottery Company measured theirs from base to rim and stamped the size on the underside of the foot. Very confusing!

For this book, all the baskets are measured from the base to the top of the handle. Pictures are misleading as to size, so listing the full height will let you know exactly what you are seeing.

Many, if not most, manufacturers made their baskets in graduated sizes, from mini-sized ones of a couple of inches, to very tall ones of more than a foot. Does size affect value? Yes and no. If you collect only miniatures, then the smaller ones are worth more to you, right? Especially if your shelf won't hold a 16″ behemoth.

How are "book" prices established? In addition to being a guide to what the market will bear, book values are a guide to replacement values. While the buyer and seller must determine the final price between themselves, book prices take into account shows, shops, flea markets, and the Internet.

When trying to determine what you personally are willing to pay, here are some things to remember:

The Internet

The Internet can be better than chocolate to buyers as well as sellers. It's pretty much open 24/7, in the worst weather, and it literally brings the world into your home.

Should Internet prices determine the value of your collection? No, no more than should a garage sale in your neighborhood. If you get lucky at a garage or tag sale, you are fortunate indeed. The same applies to the Internet. If you buy a basket for

Depression-era jade green glass basket with metal handle, #1616, Fenton Art Glass Company, 1930s, $100.00 – 125.00.

Introduction: The Basket Case

Depression-era azure blue satin glass basket with diamond optic, Fenton Art Glass Company, 1930s, $75.00 – 100.00.

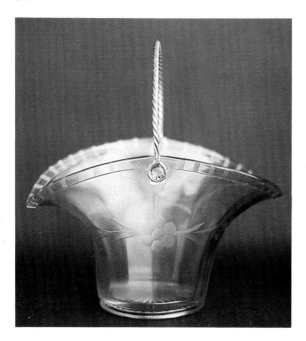

Depression-era pink glass basket with metal handle, $35.00 – 55.00.

$10.00 that books for $100.00, what are you going to insure it for? Or try to sell it for in your mall space?

Because most Internet sales of antiques and collectibles are auctions, the selling price only applies to a given day in a given transaction. The price for the same item in the next auction can be totally different.

Nobody likes to lose, so when two or more buyers get into a bidding war, the price can jump dramatically. Does that make that inflated price the true worth of the piece? Only to the person who won it! It's only what somebody was willing to pay in the excitement of the moment, the same as an in-person auction.

When an Internet auction ends, the dollar amount on the screen is final, unless there is an unmet reserve price on the item. If the reserve has not been met, the high bidder and seller are free to make a deal after the auction closes. The final price they negotiate is just between them, and you have no way of knowing how close the selling price is to the final bid on the screen.

But there are deals to be had, and Internet auctions can be very exciting and rewarding because often prices are only about half of "book" values.

Condition, Condition, Condition!

One of the benefits of in-person buying is that you and you alone determine whether the condition is acceptable. On the Internet, you are taking the seller's word for it, and it doesn't always work out the way you expect. Too often Internet sellers will list something in "perfect," "mint," or "excellent" condition when there is actually damage. Recently I saw a supposedly mint piece of glass from an Internet auction that had a lot of little rim nicks — the kind that only come with years of hard use — and when the buyer complained, the seller said, "Well, if you want to be picky about it."

That said, prices in this book are for mint condition items only — no nicks, chips, flea bites, chigger bites, scrapes, cracks, bruises, rough spots, worn spots on decorations, damaged enamel paint, or any of the myriad other euphemisms that sellers use to gloss over defects.

Where possible, the manufacturer of each basket is listed, but some of them remain unknown. Manufacturers' numbers are included when known. With more than 400 glass manufacturing companies in — and, more importantly, out of — business in the last two centuries in America alone, and nearly that many potteries, some information is just lost to the mists of time.

American Glass Baskets

Numbers in captions are factory numbers.

Boyd Glass Company • Cambridge, Ohio
1978 – Present

2¼" bushel baskets from an original Degenhart mold marked with "B in diamond," $8.00 – 12.00 each.

Cambridge Glass Company • Cambridge, Ohio
1901 – 1958

#125, Optic with light cutting (many collectors call this type of decoration "etched," but etching is done with acid, and on this piece the decoration is cut with a wheel), 9", $45.00 – 75.00.

#125, Optic with light cutting, 8¼", $45.00 – 75.00.

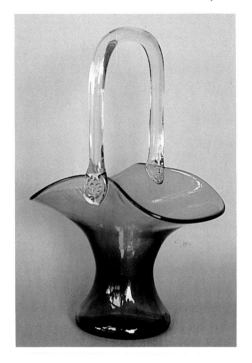

#118, emerald green, 11", $125.00 – 150.00.

#119, cobalt, 11", $175.00 – 200.00.

#118, rubina, 12", $385.00 – 400.00.

#118, amethyst (purple), 11", $125.00 – 150.00.

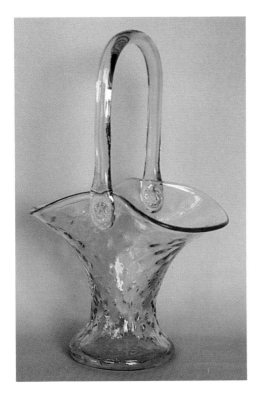

#118, willow blue aero optic, 10¾",
$750.00 – 800.00.

#118, ebony, 11", $125.00 – 150.00.

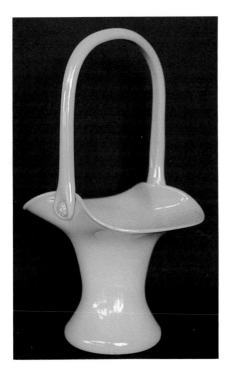

#118, special article azurite, 13½",
$265.00 – 285.00.

Helio special article favor vase, 5½",
$500.00 – 600.00.

Green Basketweave factory give-away or advertising piece, 1", $35.00 – 55.00.

Crown Tuscan Basketweave factory give-away or advertising piece, 4", $35.00 – 55.00.

Blue Basketweave factory give-away or advertising piece, 3", $35.00 – 55.00.

Clear Basketweave factory give-away or advertising pieces, left 1", right 3", $35.00 – 55.00 each.

Smoke Georgian, 6¾", $100.00 – 115.00.

Left: Elaine with gold encrustation; right: Diane with gold encrustation; 4", $200.00 – 325.00 each. Elaine and Diane are acid-etched patterns.

Dugan/Diamond Glass Company • Indiana, Pennsylvania
1904 – 1931

Left: Cobalt carnival; right: marigold carnival, 5", $35.00 – 55.00.

Left: Amethyst carnival; right: pink, 5", $35.00 – 55.00.

Left: Black; right: green, 5", $35.00 – 55.00.

Violet basket in amethyst, 6¼", $60.00 – 75.00.

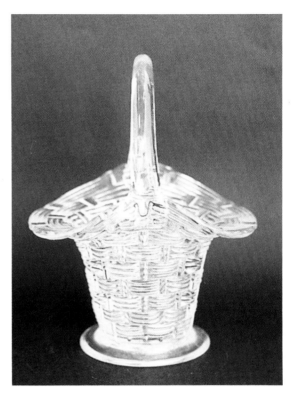

Marigold carnival basketweave, 7½", $35.00 – 55.00.

Clear basketweave, 7½", $20.00 – 35.00.

Marigold crackle, a.k.a. Tree of Life, 6", $30.00 – 40.00.

Marigold carnival basketweave, 5¾", $30.00 – 40.00.

Duncan/Duncan Miller
Pittsburgh, Pennsylvania (1865 – 1893) and Washington, Pennsylvania (1893 – 1955)

Tavern is the classic early twentieth century basket shape, and the shape was used with variations by several glass companies including Duncan. Most of Duncan's baskets in this shape have a notch on each side of the rim, and often have "PAT'D" or "PAT PEND" molded into the inside bottom. Some of Duncan's souvenir and other baskets are very similar to Westmoreland's, but the Duncan products have a panel line under each side of the handle, while the Westmoreland products have a large, flat panel with no line.

Tavern with light cutting (the bands were in the mold), 9¾", $55.00 – 75.00.

Larger tavern, 11¾", "PAT'D" molded in bottom, $65.00 – 85.00.

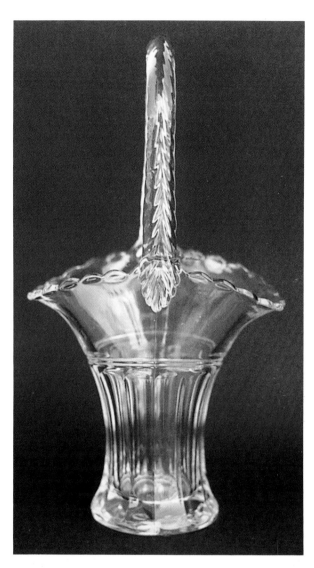

Medium-sized tavern, 9¾", $45.00 – 65.00.

Small tavern, 6", "PAT'D" molded in bottom, $20.00 – 30.00.

Paneled with light cutting, 5", "PAT'D" molded in bottom, $35.00 – 45.00.

Paneled, 13", "PAT'D" molded in bottom, $60.00 – 80.00.

Left: Paneled with light cutting, 6½", "PAT'D" molded in bottom, $35.00 – 45.00; right: paneled with light cutting, 6½", $35.00 – 45.00.

Paneled, 11½", "PAT'D" molded in bottom, $65.00 – 85.00.

Paneled, 12", "PAT'D" molded in bottom, $65.00 – 85.00.

Complete centerpiece set of seven matched baskets, paneled with light cutting, large one is 11½", "PAT'D" molded in bottom, $175.00 – 225.00 set.

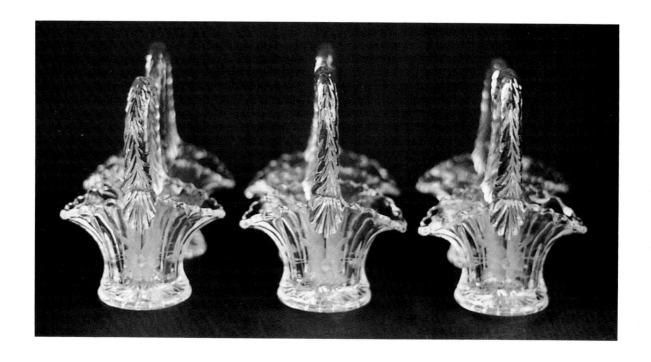

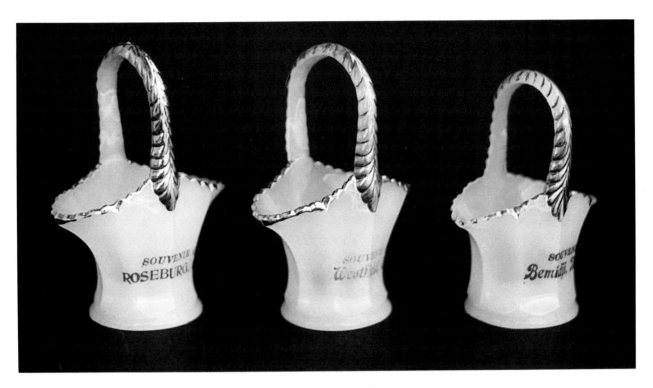

Clambroth souvenirs. Left to right: Roseburg, 5"; Westfield, 5"; Bemidji, 4½"; $35.00 – 45.00 each.

Clambroth souvenirs. Left to right: St. Anthony, 5"; Kenmarc, 4¼"; ruby souvenir Machlas, 4½"; $35.00 – 45.00 each.

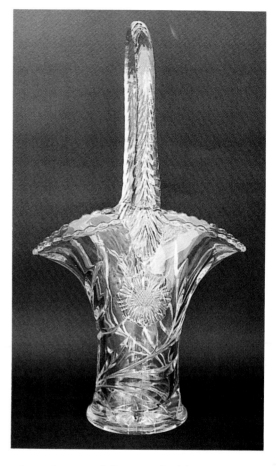

**Left: #118, Caribbean blue opalescent hobnail, 10¾",
$130.00 – 200.00; right: #118, clear hobnail, 9½", $65.00
– 85.00.**

Crystal, pressed flower, 16", $45.00 – 55.00.

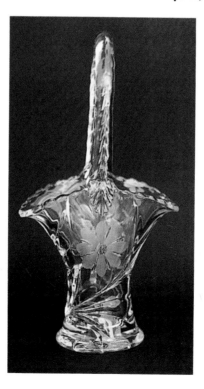

**Clear, pressed with light cutting, 10",
$55.00 – 65.00.**

**Amber, pressed flower, 10", $65.00 –
85.00.**

#41, Early American Sandwich pattern, 4¾", $85.00 – 125.00.

#41, Early American Sandwich pattern, 11½", $200.00 – 250.00.

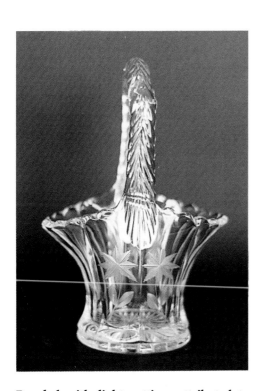

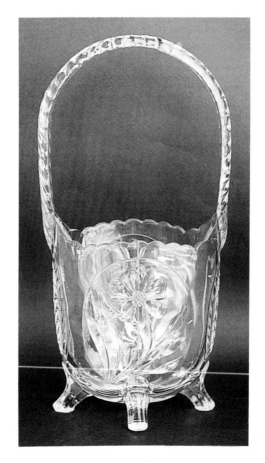

Paneled with light cutting, attributed to Duncan, 6½", $35.00 – 45.00.

Pressed footed, 12", $200.00 – 250.00.

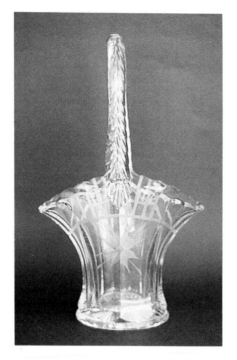

Paneled with light cutting, attributed to Duncan, 9¾", $55.00 – 75.00.

Paneled with light cutting, attributed to Duncan, 9¾", $55.00 – 75.00.

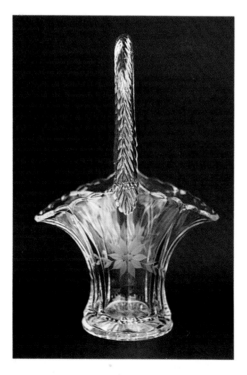

Paneled with light cutting, attributed to Duncan, 12", $55.00 – 75.00.

Paneled with light cutting, attributed to Duncan, 13¼", $55.00 – 75.00.

**Plain, paneled, attributed to Duncan, 9½",
$45.00 – 65.00.**

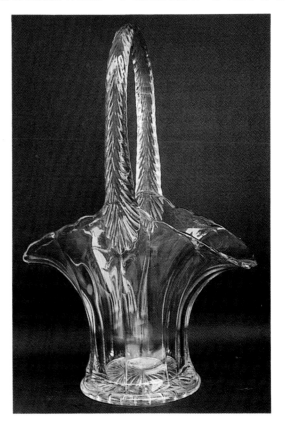

**Plain, paneled, attributed to Duncan, 13½",
$60.00 – 80.00.**

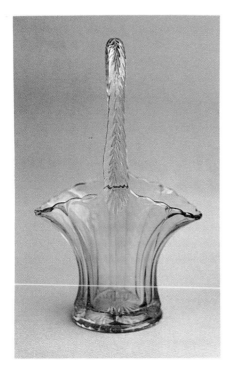

Amber, paneled, attributed to Duncan, 10", $40.00 – 60.00.

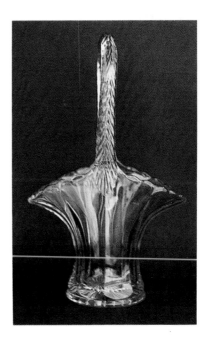

Pink, paneled, attributed to Duncan, 12¼", $75.00 – $85.00.

#115, Canterbury, Cape Cod blue opalescent, 10",
$75.00 – 85.00.

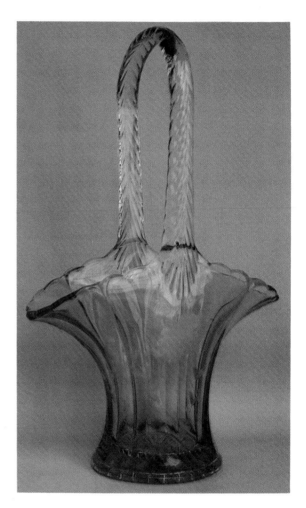

Pink, paneled with light cutting, attributed to
Duncan, 12½", $85.00 – 100.00.

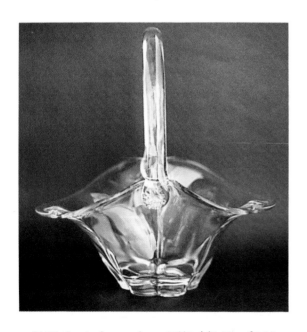

#115, Canterbury, clear, 10½", $45.00 – 65.00.

#115, Canterbury, cranberry pink opalescent, 9½", $80.00 – 90.00.

#115, Canterbury, Cape Cod blue opalescent, 10", $75.00 – 85.00.

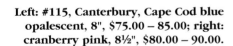

Left: #115, Canterbury, Cape Cod blue opalescent, 8", $75.00 – 85.00; right: cranberry pink, 8½", $80.00 – 90.00.

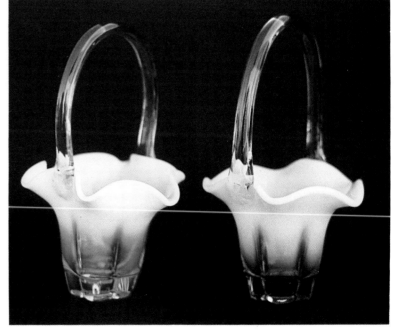

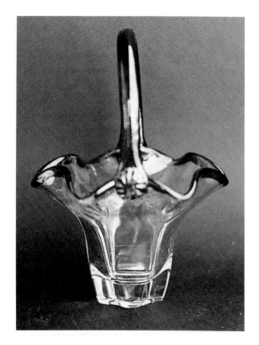

#115, Canterbury, clear with red iridized
rim, 5½", $115.00 – 125.00.

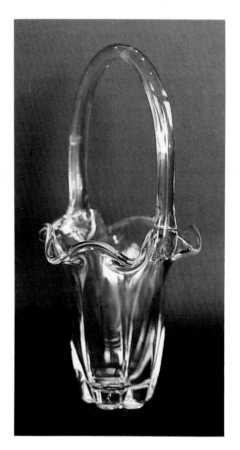

#115, Canterbury, clear, 10", $45.00 –
60.00.

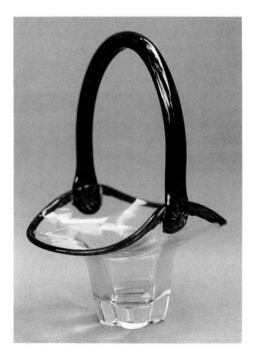

#115, Canterbury, clear with red iridized
rim, $115.00 – 125.00.

Fenton Art Glass Company • Williamstown, West Virginia
1906 – Present

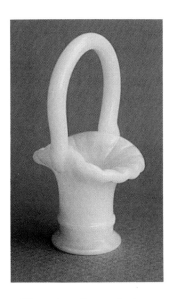

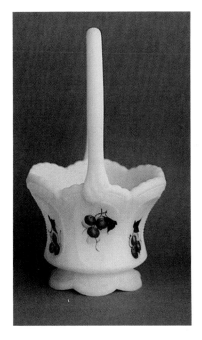

Milk (opal) miniature 1980s, 4", $45.00 – 60.00. (Although white opaque glassware has always been sold as "milk glass," it was usually called "opal," pronounced o-PÁL, by glassmakers.)

Milk (opal) satin, hand-painted Bayberry, made from a votive candle mold, 1980s, $30.00 – 40.00. (Christmas baskets such as this one were offered for one season only.)

Left: Grape miniature, 5"; right: blue opalescent, 4½", both with silver label; $20.00 – 40.00 each.

**Beatty Waffle reproduction, blue opalescent, 8¾",
1960s, $40.00 – 60.00.**

**Gloss Burmese, 6", 1991, a sample item,
$145.00 – 155.00.**

**Burmese Queensware, hand painted
by Connie Ash, 1970s, 7¼", $125.00 –
145.00.**

**Butterfly & Berry. Left: Pink stretch velva rose, 8", 1980s, $50.00 – 60.00;
right: cobalt, 8", 1980s, molded with Fenton oval (only made for a few
years), $40.00 – 45.00.**

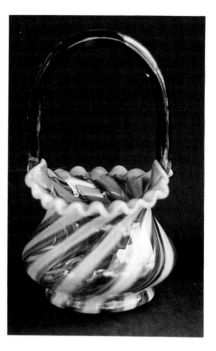

Cactus, blue opalescent, 8½", late 1980s, molded with small Fenton oval, $85.00 – 95.00.

Cameo opalescent spiral, 8", 1970s, molded with large Fenton oval, $50.00 – 65.00.

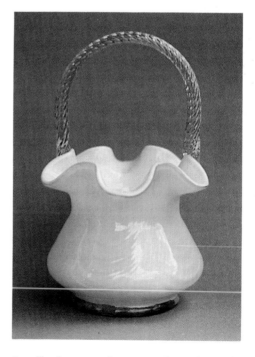

Cameo satin "Down by the Station," 8", 1983, an unusual decoration, not in the regular Fenton line, hand painted by Dana Frederick, $85.00 – 95.00.

Candleglow, amber cased with milk (opal), 8", $75.00 – 85.00.

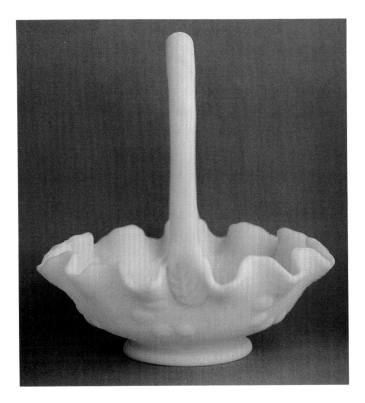

Cherries, lime sherbet, 1960s, 8½", $28.00 – 35.00.

Coin Dot, blue cased with milk (opal), 7", 1940s – 50s, $85.00 – 100.00. (The difference between Coin Dot and Coin Spot is that you can see through the dots, and you can't through the spots. Some other glass companies used the name Polka Dot instead of Coin Dot.)

Coin Dot, all 5¾". Left to right: Cranberry 1940s – 50s, $85.00 – 95.00; French opalescent, 1940s – 1950s, $45.00 – 50.00; Persian blue, one year only, 1989, molded with Fenton oval, $50.00 – 60.00.

Connoisseur Collection, 8¾", 1980s, $85.00 – $110.00.

Oval English basket, milk (opal), 3¾", 1960s, $18.00 – 20.00.

Oval English baskets. Left: Colonial blue, 3¾", $25.00 – 35.00; right: colonial amber, 3¾", $18.00 – 28.00.

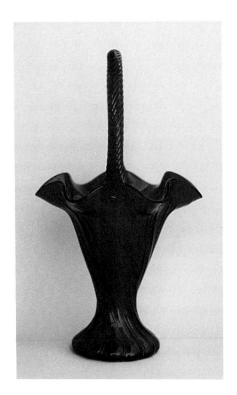

Cobalt, 11½", 1980s, $70.00 – 85.00.

Silver Crest, 10¾", with paper label, 1980s – 90s, $85.00; if older with no logo $125.00.

Silver Crest, 7¾", $40.00 – 45.00.

Silver Crest, 7½", 1950s – 60s, $40.00 – 50.00.

Left: Silver Crest, 7¼", $30.00 – 50.00; right: Silver Crest, 6¾", $30.00 – 50.00.

Left: Silver Crest with forget-me-nots, 7", year, $45.00 – 65.00; right: Silver Crest DV (Decorated Violets, called "Violets in the Snow" by collectors), 6¾", $45.00 – 65.00.

Apple Blossom (crest is opaque pink, made for only two to three years in the 1960s), 7", $125.00 – 150.00.

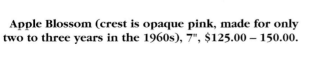
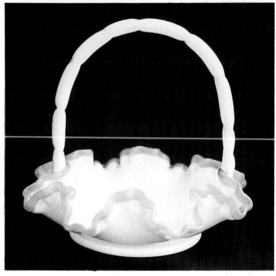

Peach Crest, 8", 1950s, $75.00 – 85.00.

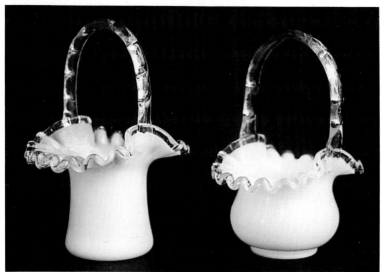

Left: Peach Crest, 7", 1950s, $50.00 – 60.00;
right: Aqua Crest, 6½", 1940s, $60.00 – 70.00.

Left: Gold Crest, 7", 1940s and 1960s,
$45.00 – 55.00; right: Gold Crest 7½",
1940s and 1960s, $45.00 – 55.00.

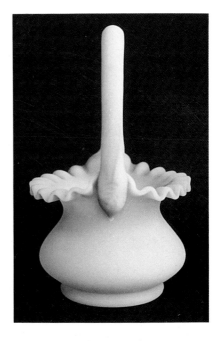

Silver rose (rose pastel with a crystal edge or crest), 8",
1940s, $45.00 – 60.00.

Left: Green overlay with milk (opal), 6¼",
1950s, $55.00 – 65.00; right: Burmese,
6¾", $65.00 – 85.00.

QVC item signed "WC Fenton," Daisy & Fern, 9¼", 1990s, originally $41.00,
$75.00 – 85.00.

Embossed roses (from a Dugan mold), 7½",
1960s, $40.00 – 50.00.

Threaded diamond optic, wisteria, 8¼", 1970s,
molded with large Fenton in oval logo, $75.00
– 85.00.

Strawberries, French opalescent, 7¼", 1970s,
molded with small Fenton in oval logo, $40.00
– 50.00.

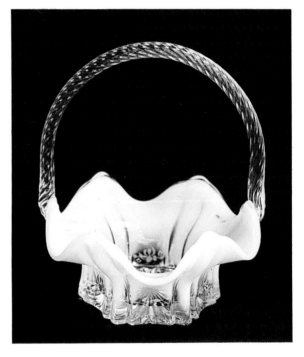

Hand-painted French opalescent, 8", 1980s, probably from an Easter collection, $45.00 – 50.00.

Hanging Heart, 7", 1970s, $145.00 – 185.00.

Hanging Heart, 11", 1970s, $250.00 – 300.00.

Hobnail, colonial green, 7½", 1960s, $30.00 – 35.00.

Hobnail, topaz opalescent, 10¾", 1950s – 60s, $170.00 – 195.00.

Hobnail, cranberry opalescent, 9¼", 1950s – 60s, $185.00 – 205.00.

Hobnail, blue opalescent, 10½", 1950s – 60s, $150.00 – 170.00.

Hobnail, milk (opal), 6½", made for at least 30 years, $25.00 – 30.00.

Hobnail, cranberry opalescent, 8", 1990s, the method of crimping the rim is their newer style, $85.00 – 100.00.

Hobnail, blue opalescent, 7½", 1950s, the crimping on this one is their older style, $65.00 – 75.00.

Hobnail, ruby, 7½", 1972 – 1984, $50.00 – 60.00.

Hobnail, French opalescent, 5½", 1950s – 60s, $35.00 – 40.00.

Hobnail, rose pastel, 6½", 1950s, $45.00 – 55.00.

Left: Hobnail, pink opalescent, 6", 1980s, molded with small Fenton in oval logo, $50.00 – 60.00; right: Hobnail, topaz opalescent, 6", 1980s, molded with large Fenton in oval logo, $80.00 – 90.00.

Left: Hobnail, topaz opalescent, 6", $65.00 – 75.00; right: Hobnail, blue opalescent, 5½", 1950s – 60s, $45.00 – 60.00.

Hobnail, cranberry opalescent, 5½", 1930s, $65.00 – 75.00.

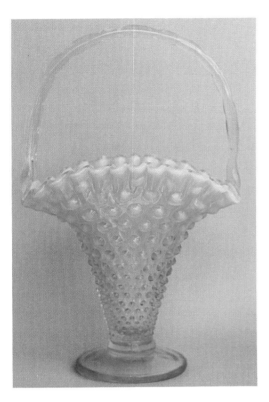

Hobnail, blue opalescent, 9", $75.00 – 85.00.

Lily of the Valley, 7½", 1990s, $35.00 – 40.00.

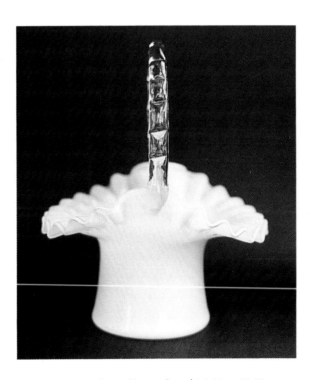

Rose overlay, 8½", 1940s, $35.00 – 50.00.

Left: Blue overlay with single crimped edge, 6½", 1950s, $50.00 – 60.00; right: ruby overlay with double crimped edge, 6½", 1990s, with Fenton oval paper label, $75.00 – 95.00.

Mulberry #1432, 7½", 1989, $75.00 – 95.00.　　**Regency, federal blue, 7¼", 1980s, $25.00 – 35.00.**

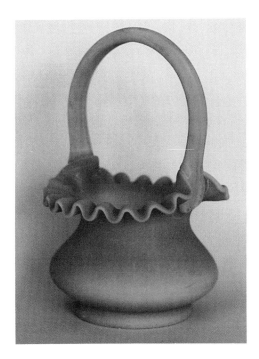

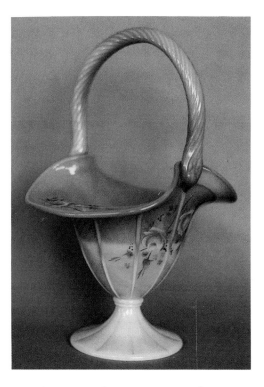

Rose satin, 7", 1970s (not a lot were made with the same colored handle), $50.00 – 70.00.

QVC item, Rosalene, 11", 1992, $125.00 – 145.00.

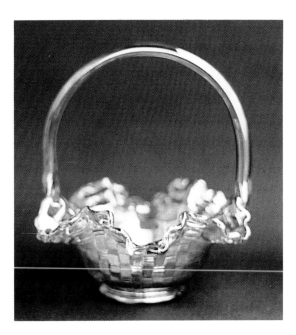

Open Edge Basketweave, teal carnival (Fenton calls it "Teal Marigold"), 7", 1980s, molded with small Fenton in oval logo, $40.00 – 45.00.

Thumbprint, 8", 1960s – 70s, came both signed and unsigned, $40.00 – 45.00.

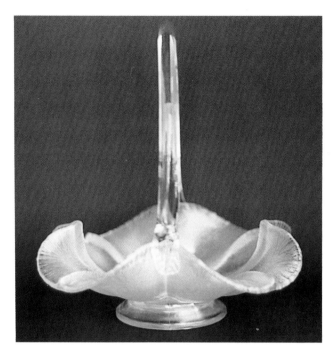

Blue overlay melon (short melon), 8", 1940s – 50s, $55.00 – 65.00.

Blue stretch, 8", 1980s, $95.00 – 105.00.

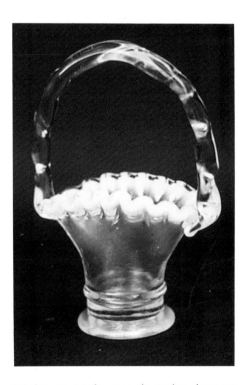

Miniature, opalescent, 4", 1940s, $100.00 – 135.00.

Limited-edition stretch black, 4¼", 1978, only 1,000 made, $135.00 – 160.00.

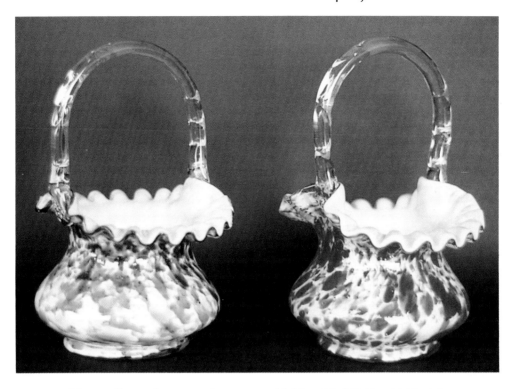

Vasa Murrhina, 1960s. Left: Aventurine green with blue, 7", $60.00 – 85.00; right: autumn orange, 7", $60.00 – 85.00.

Vasa Murrhina, rose mist, 11", 1960s, $175.00 – 195.00.

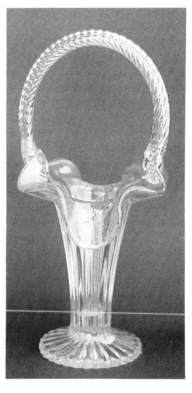

Cone-shaped basket vase, 9", 1999, with paper oval Fenton label, $25.00 – 45.00.

American Glass Baskets

Gibson Glass • Milton, West Virginia
1976 – 1977; 1983 – Present

Gibsons are usually molded with their name and the year of production.

Cobalt carnival, with daisy, 7½", 1988, $25.00 – 35.00.

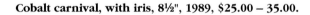

Cobalt carnival, with iris, 8½", 1989, $25.00 – 35.00.

Left: Red carnival, 4¼", 1989, $12.00 – 18.00; right: cobalt carnival, 3¼", 1990, $12.00 – 18.00.

Left to right: Cobalt, 4½", 1989, $12.00 – 18.00; cobalt carnival, 4½", no date, but purchased in 1990, $12.00 – 18.00; green, 4½", no date, but purchased in 1990, $12.00 – 18.00.

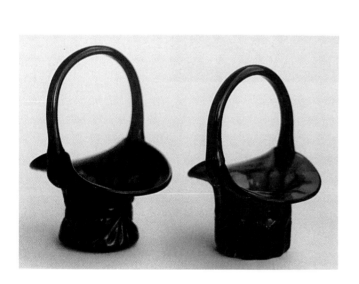

Left: Red, 4½", 1989, $15.00 – 25.00; right: cobalt, 4½", no date, $15.00 – 25.00.

Cobalt, 7", 1990, $15.00 – 25.00.

A.H. Heisey Glass Company • Newark, Ohio
1893 – 1956

Heisey frequently marked their pieces with their logo, an H inside a diamond. Heisey's earlier baskets have rings on each side of the handle just above where it joins the body; the later ones do not. Heisey's older handles have a ground and polished flattened spot on top of the handle where the glass was pushed into the mold, then later polished out. Heisey measured their baskets from lip to lip, so, for instance, the #465 Recessed Panel 8" basket is actually 11" tall.

#460, Pinwheel & Fan, 11¾", $350.00 – 400.00. (A reproduction of this has been showing up in the Midwest in vaseline yellow, pink, and green.)

#1404, Old Sandwich whimsey, 7¼", $900.00 – 1,100.00. (One of four or five known. Whimsies were made by workmen on their lunch hours or after work, usually for personal use or as gifts, and were not included in the factory's line.)

Light cutting, 11¾", $225.00 – 250.00.

#462, Plain Hexagon, common name used by collectors, 11", $180.00 – 200.00.

#473 with deep etching #342, 11¾", $350.00 – 400.00.

#465, Recessed Panel, common name used by collectors, 10¼", $200.00 – 225.00.

#465, Recessed Panel with non-factory flower frog, 11", $225.00 – 250.00.

#465, satin glass Recessed Panel, 11", $225.00 – 250.00.

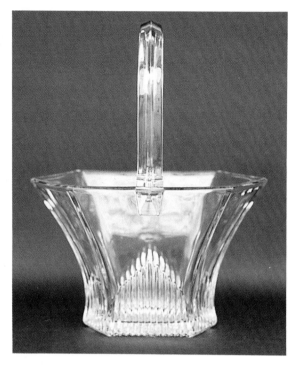

#458, Picket, common name used by collectors, 10½", $250.00 – 275.00.

#458, Picket with light cutting, 10¾", $250.00 – 325.00.

#461, Banded Picket, common name used by collectors, Flamingo, 9¼", $350.00 – 400.00.

#461, Banded Picket, Moongleam, 10½", $375.00 – 425.00. (Moongleam is a much rarer color.)

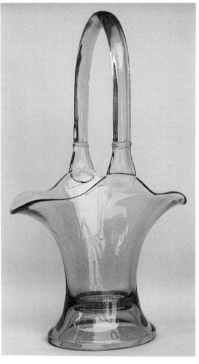

#463, Bonnet, common name used by collectors, Flamingo, 13½", $425.00 – 500.00.

#463 Bonnet, with enamel and gold decoration, 13¼", $445.00 – 525.00.

#463, Bonnet with cutting, 15½", $250.00 – 300.00.

#477, Hairpin, common name used by collectors, 16", $700.00 – 750.00.

#417, Double Rib & Panel, common name used by collectors, Hawthorne, 8¼", $350.00 – 450.00.

#417, Double Rib & Panel, Moongleam, 8¼", $300.00 – 325.00.

#417, Double Rib & Panel with light cutting, 8¼", $190.00 – 225.00.

#1503, Crystolite, 8½", $350.00 – 400.00.

#464, Fruit basket with light cutting, 10",
$250.00 – 275.00.

#466, Fruit basket with light cutting, $250.00 –
275.00.

#466, Fruit basket with light cutting, $250.00 – 275.00.

#459, Round Colonial, common name used by collectors, with blue cut to clear, 15½", $550.00 – 600.00.

#459, Round Colonial with deep etching #352, 14", $325.00 – 350.00.

#459, Round Colonial with light cutting, 13", $325.00 – 350.00. (Amber bands are reflections, not color in the glass.)

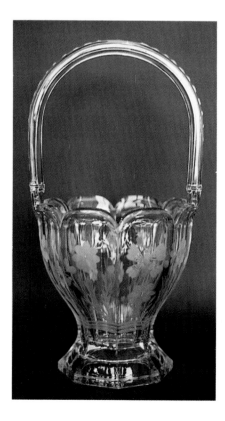

#459, Round Colonial with light cutting, 13", $325.00 – 350.00. (Amber bands are reflections, not color in the glass.)

#500, Octagon, common name used by collectors, 4¾"; left: marigold, $300.00 – 325.00; right: clear, $100.00 – 125.00.

#467, Helmet, common name used by collectors, in Flamingo, 10¾", $1,500.00 – 2,000.00.

Lariat, 10", $300.00 – 350.00.

Lariat, loops are down, 5", $200.00 – 250.00.

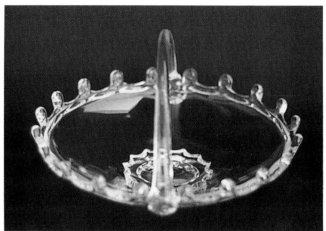

Lariat, loops are up, 5", $150.00 – 175.00.

Lariat, loops are up and sides are curved, 6¼", $165.00 – 185.00.

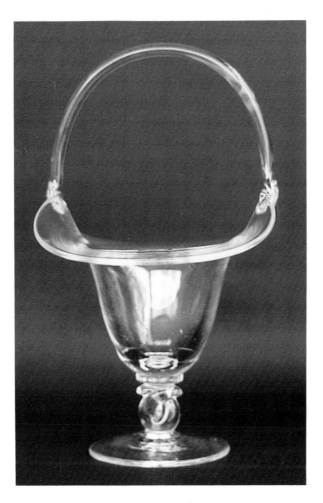

Lariat, no loops, 9", $175.00 – 200.00.

Orchid, 10", on Lariat blank, no loops, $1,250.00 – 1,500.00.

Imperial Glass Company • Bellaire, Ohio
1901/1904 – 1985

#698, Monticello in marigold carnival, 10", $100.00 – 125.00.

Slim, narrow panels, 10½", $45.00 – 65.00.

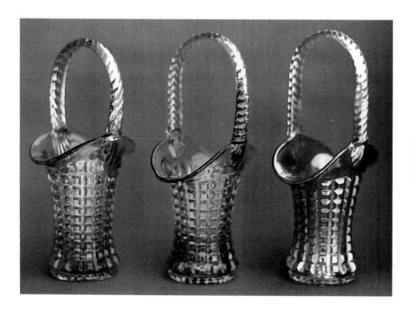

#698, Monticello. Left to right: Pink, 9¼", $85.00 – 125.00; blue, 9", $85.00 – 125.00; marigold carnival, 9½", $100.00 – 135.00.

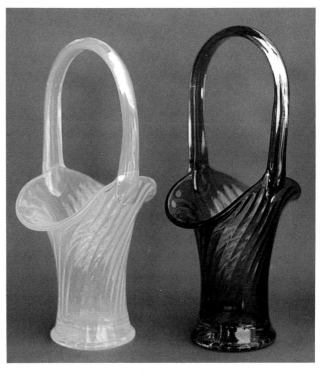

#313, Twisted Optic, common name used by collectors from Hazel Marie Weatherman, 10". Left: Amber, $60.00 – 85.00; right: green, $85.00 – $125.00.

#313, Twisted Optic, 10". Left: Golden Green (called vaseline by collectors), $90.00 – 130.00; right: Rose Marie (pink), $85.00 – 125.00.

#714, Grape in milk (opal) with gold, 9½", $45.00 – 65.00.

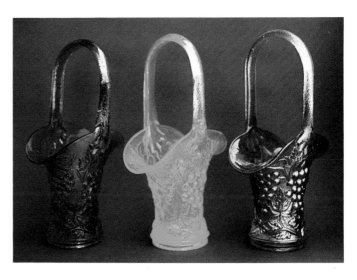

#714, Grape. Left to right: Rose Marie (pink), 10", $85.00 – 125.00; green, 10", $85.00 – 125.00; right: rubigold carnival, 10", $100.00 – 135.00.

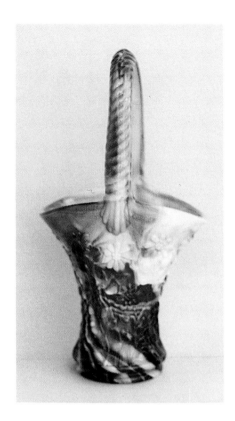

#40, Daisy in caramel slag, 10", IG logo molded in base, $80.00 – 95.00.

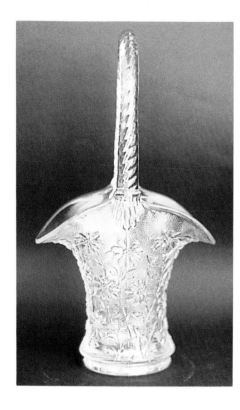

#40, Daisy in clear, 10½", $35.00 – 40.00.

#1950/40, Daisy, 10". Left to right: Peacock (or amber) carnival, reissue 1980s, $50.00 – 85.00; azure blue carnival, reissue 1970s, $50.00 – 85.00; marigold carnival, original, purchased in 1942, $100.00 – 150.00.

#160/221, Cape Cod, 10", $150.00 – $200.00.

#252, Rose Marie (pink), 14", $85.00 – 125.00.

#300, iridescent blue stretch, 10", $85.00 – 125.00.

Imperial and Tiffin produced baskets so similar that the only way to tell them apart is by the colors and the feet. Imperial's have pronounced foot rings, as seen in this close-up; Tiffin's do not.

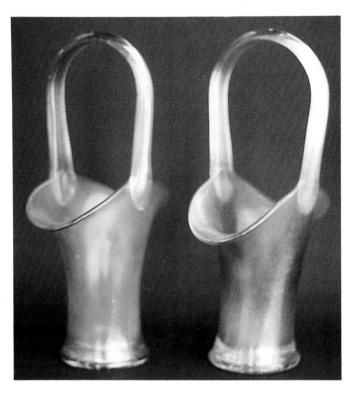

Left: Iridescent blue stretch, 10", $85.00 – 125.00; right: marigold carnival stretch, 1¼", $100.00 – 150.00.

#300, ruby slag, 10¼", label "Olden End o' Day Glass by Imperial" and IG molded in base, $80.00 – 95.00.

#475, ruby slag. Left: Satin finish, 4", $40.00 – 50.00; right: glossy finish, $40.00 – 50.00.

#156, ruby slag, glossy finish, 4¾", "IG" molded in base, $30.00 – 35.00.

Blue milk glass, 5", "IG" molded in base, $30.00 – 35.00.

Milk (opal) glass, 4¾", "IG" molded in base, $25.00 – 30.00.

#368, milk (opal) glass, 4¾", $20.00 – 30.00.

Indiana Glass Company • Dunkirk, Indiana
1904 – Present

Crystal with silver, new in 1977, 7¾", $20.00 – 30.00.

#1008, Willow, Oleander, reputed factory names, clear with ruby flash, 10½", $125.00 – 140.00.

Clear with multicolored flash, 1970s, 5", $40.00 – 45.00.

Garland with ruby flash, 10½", $40.00 – 45.00.

Kanawha • Dunbar, West Virginia
1957 – 1987

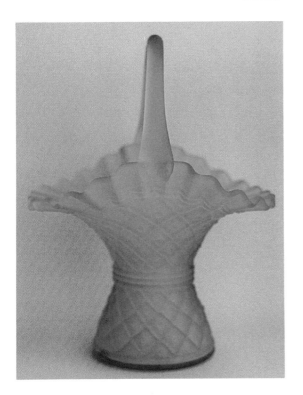

Blue satin, 8½", $25.00 – 35.00.

Ruby with clear handle, 10", $30.00 – 40.00.

Milk (opal) Hobnail, 7½", attributed to Kanawha, $12.00 – 20.00.

Hobnail opaque, 6¾", foil label "Kanawha Hand Crafted Glassware, Dunbar, W VA," $20.00 – 30.00.

Blue Hobnail, 6", attributed to Kanawha, $12.00 – 20.00.

Green slag, 4½", attributed to Kanawha, $12.00 – 20.00.

Milk (opal) satin. Left: Cased with blue, 3", $15.00 – 20.00; right: cased with yellow, $15.00 – 20.00.

Left: Amber with 12 panels, 5", attributed to Kanawha, $12.00 – 18.00; right: ruby, 5½", paper label "Kanawha Hand Crafted Glassware, Dunbar, W VA," $15.00 – 25.00.

Crackle, paper label "Kanawha Hand Crafted Glassware, Dunbar, W VA." Left: Blue, 4½", $15.00 – 25.00; right: orange, 4½", $15.00 – 25.00.

Ruby crackle, 6", $15.00 – 30.00.

Blue crackle, 4½", attributed to Kanawha, $15.00 – 25.00.

McKee Glass Company • Jeannette, Pennsylvania
1904 – 1951

Priscilla, 8", $60.00 – 65.00.

Martec Prescut in milk (opal), 6", reissue, $20.00 – 35.00.

Morgantown • Morgantown, West Virginia
1899 – 1972

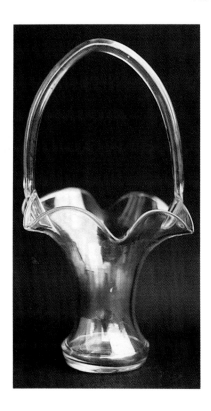

Patrick iridescent, 10½", attributed to Morgantown, body is like their Patrick, but handle is different from catalogs, $45.00 – 65.00.

Mosser Glass • Cambridge, Ohio
1959 – Present

Georgian, cobalt, 4¼", molded with M in base, $15.00 – 25.00.

Miniature Georgian, $18.00 – 28.00.

Left: Amethyst, 8", molded with M in base, $18.00 – 28.00; right: cobalt, 7¼", molded with M in base, $18.00 – 28.00.

New Martinsville Glass Manufacturing Company • New Martinsville, West Virginia
1901 – 1944

Janice, 8½", $60.00 – 70.00.

Greek Key, 5½", New Martinsville logo molded in base, $35.00 – 50.00.

Janice, clear with red handle, 8½", $125.00 – 135.00.

Janice, red with clear handle, 9½", $165.00 – 195.00.

Northwood • Wheeling, West Virginia
1896 – 1923

Left: Black basketweave, 4½"; right: iridescent carnival, "N" molded inside base, $50.00 – 75.00 each.

L.E. Smith • Mt. Pleasant, Pennsylvania
1907 – Present

Feather, black with clear handle, 12", $125.00 – 150.00.

L.E. Smith reproduction of McKee innovation, blue carnival, 12¼", $25.00 – 40.00.

#1136, 10", circa 1979, $25.00 – 40.00.

#637, Dominion, 10½", $25.00 – 40.00.

Tiara • Indiana Glass Company • Dunkirk, Indiana
1970 – 1998

Coral Empress, a reproduction of McKee's Bird of Paradise, peach, 7", $20.00 – 30.00. (You can tell the reproduction from the original by the color – the originals are pink; the reproductions are coral, a peachier color.)

Tearose Windmill, 12", $35.00 – 50.00.

Dogwood, 6", handler's mark "CB," $35.00 – 40.00.

Reissue of Indiana Garland, 11", $35.00 – 40.00.

Tiffin • U.S. Glass • Tiffin, Ohio
1887 – 1962

#310, favor baskets. Left to right: Amberina satin with rope handle, 4", $50.00 – 70.00; amberina with rope handle, 3½", $35.00 – 55.00; amber with plain handle, 4", $35.00 – 55.00.

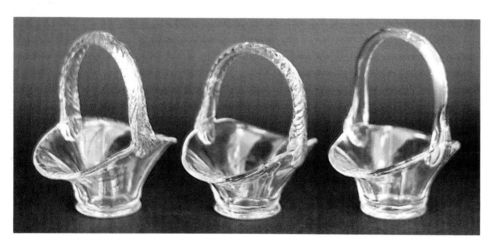

#310, favor baskets. Left to right: Clear with rope handle, 3¾"; rose pink with rope handle, 3½"; rose pink with plain handle, 4", $35.00 – 55.00 each.

#310, favor baskets. Left: Cobalt with plain handle, 4"; right: black satin with rope handle, 4", $35.00 – 55.00 each.

#310, favor baskets. Left: Sky blue satin with rope handle, 3¾"; right: sky blue with rope handle, 3¾", $35.00 – 55.00 each.

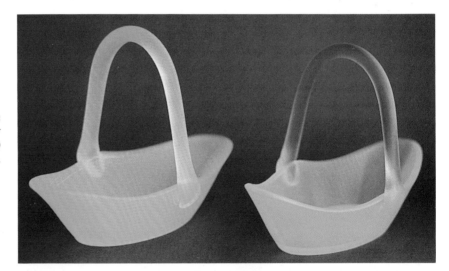

#15151, serving or art baskets. Left: Reflex green satin, 5½"; right: canary yellow vaseline, 5", $35.00 – 55.00 each.

#15151, larger serving or art basket with light cutting, 6¾", $45.00 – 55.00.

#15151, serving or art basket, 5", $35.00 – 45.00.

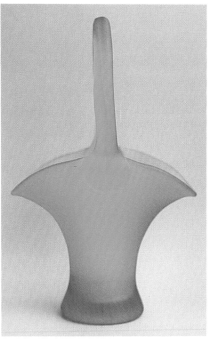

#9574, emerald green satin, 10½", $85.00 – 125.00.

#9574, black satin with gold decoration, 10½", $100.00 – 150.00.

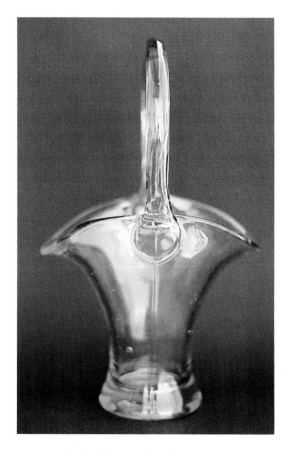

#9574, sky blue, 10½", $85.00 – 125.00.

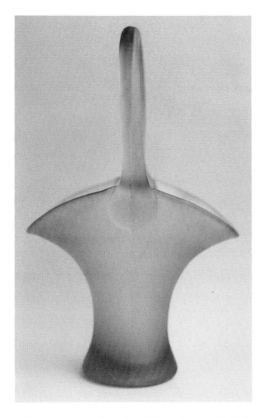

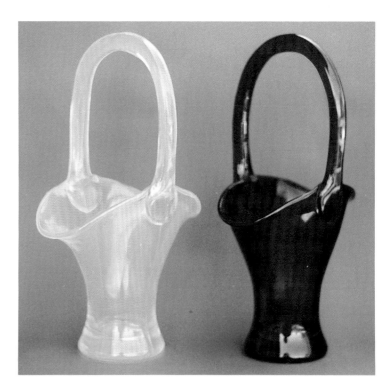

#9574, rose pink satin, 11", $85.00 – 125.00.

#9574. Left: Canary yellow vaseline, 11"; right: amberina, 11", $85.00 – 125.00 each.

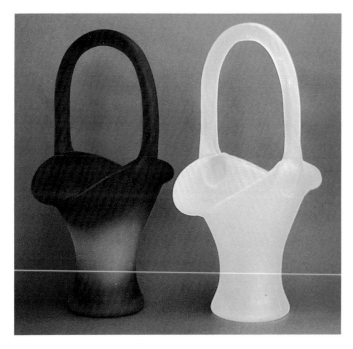

#9574. Left: Amberina satin, 11", $85.00 – 125.00; right: canary yellow vaseline satin, 11½", $85.00 – 125.00 each.

#9574. Left: Amberina satin, 10¾"; right: black satin, 11½", $85.00 – 125.00 each.

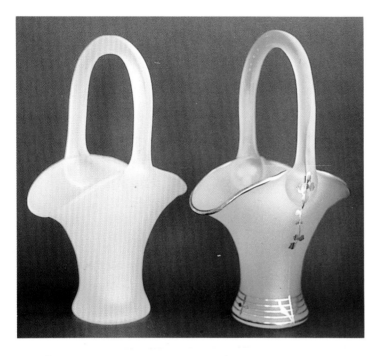

#9574. Left: Reflex green satin, 10¾", $85.00 – 125.00; right: sky blue satin with silver overlay, 11", $100.00 – 150.00.

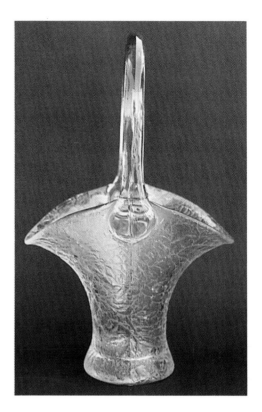

#9574, Jack Frost, 11", $85.00 – 125.00.

#310, amberina, 10½", $85.00 – 125.00.

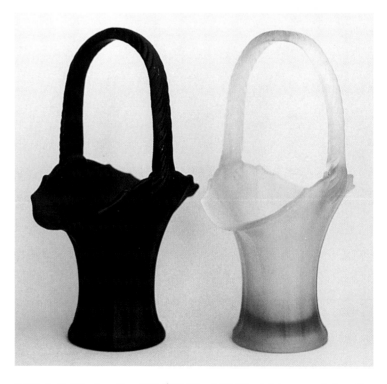

#310. Left: Black satin, 10", $85.00 – 125.00; right: rose pink satin, 10", $85.00 – 125.00.

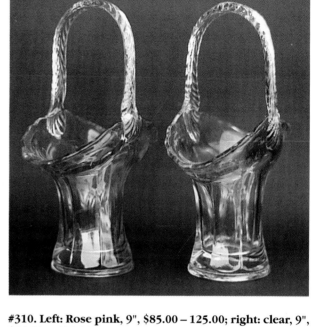

#310. Left: Rose pink, 9", $85.00 – 125.00; right: clear, 9", $85.00 – 125.00.

#310. Left: Sky blue, 9", $85.00 – 125.00; right: reflex green, 9", $85.00 – 125.00.

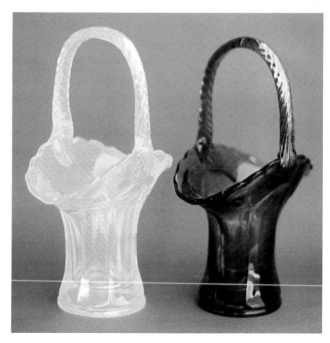

#310. Left: Canary yellow, 9½", $85.00 – 125.00; right: amber, 9", $60.00 – 85.00.

#9581, clear with light cutting, 9¾", $55.00 – 75.00.

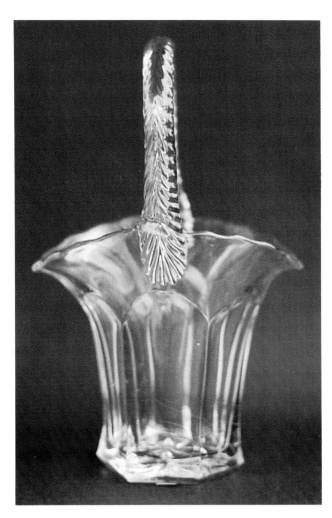

#9581, clear, 9½", $45.00 – 65.00.

#9566, clear with light cutting, 8½", $55.00 – 75.00.

#15165, clear with light cutting, 10", $55.00 – 75.00.

#9576, clear with light cutting, 11", $350.00 – 400.00.

#15308, clear, 10", $25.00 – 45.00.

U.S. Glass, "Galloway," c. 1902, 10", $200.00 – 250.00.

Viking • New Martinsville, West Virginia
1950s – 1998

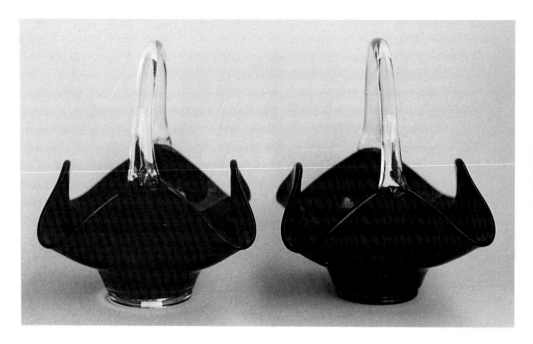

Left: Amberina-type, 6½"; right: ruby, 6½", label "Viking Hand Made," $20.00 – 40.00 each.

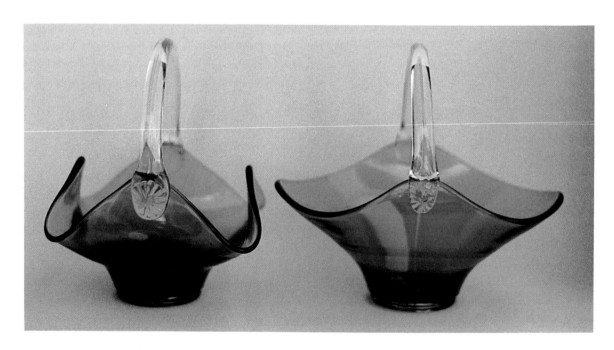

Left: Blue, with edges upturned, 6½"; right: blue, 6½", $20.00 – 40.00 each.

Amber, 6¼", $15.00 – 20.00.

Blue, 7½", $25.00 – 45.00.

Amber, 7½", $15.00 – 25.00.

Green, 5½", $20.00 – 40.00.

Ruby, 6½", $30.00 – 40.00.

Green, 9¼", $20.00 – 40.00.

Viking's reissue of New Martinsville's Krystal Klear line basket, 8½", $85.00 – 95.00.

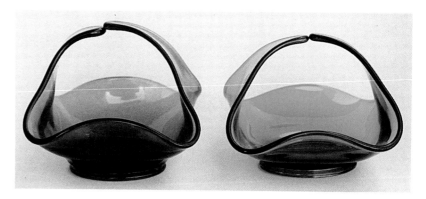

Left: Amethyst, 4½"; right: blue, 4", $20.00 – 30.00 each.

Westmoreland Glass Company • Grapeville, Pennsylvania
1890 – 1985

Westmoreland's and Duncan's paneled baskets are very close in appearance. The panel under the handle on each side of Westmoreland's basket is not clearly divided, making it look like one large, nearly flat panel. This is clearly seen in the photo at the bottom left. Duncan's have sharply defined, even panels all around. Some of Westmoreland's souvenir and other baskets are very similar to Duncan products, but the Duncans have a panel line under each side of the handle, while the Westmoreland products have a large, flat panel with no line.

Left: #750, clear with light cutting, 8¾", $55.00 – 75.00.

Right: #750, clear with acid etching, 9½", $55.00 – 75.00.

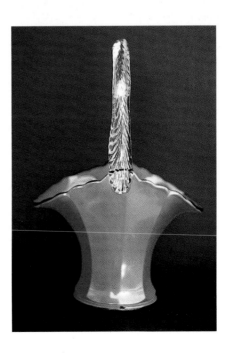

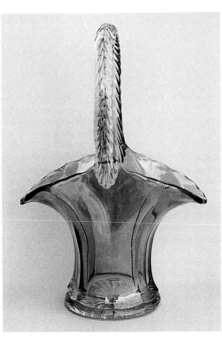

Left: #750, clear with lavender flash, 9", $45.00 – 55.00.

Right: #750, clear with orange and black fired-on enamel, 12", $65.00 – 85.00.

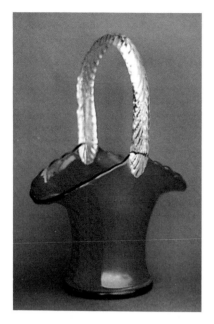

#750, clear with orange and black fired-on enamel, 9½", $45.00 – 55.00.

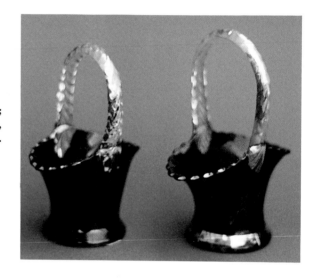

#750. Left: Clear with ruby flashing, 4¾", $20.00 – 30.00;
right: souvenir, clear with ruby flashing, "Mother," 5¼",
$35.00 – 45.00.

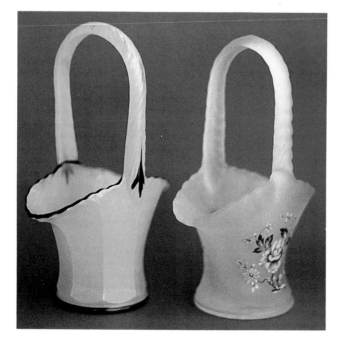

#750. Left: Clear with yellow and black fired-on enamel,
6", $35.00 – 45.00; right: white satin with flower decal,
6½", $20.00 – 30.00.

#750. Left: Green, 9½", $85.00 – 125.00; right: clear with blue flashing, 8¾", $85.00 – 125.00.

#750. Left to right: Pink, 10"; blue, 10"; green, 9½", $85.00 – 125.00 each.

#750, black shiny, 6", $40.00 – 60.00.

#750, 1970s – 1980s. Left: Pink mist satin with daisy decal, 6½", $20.00 – 30.00; right: amber satin, 6½", $15.00 – 25.00.

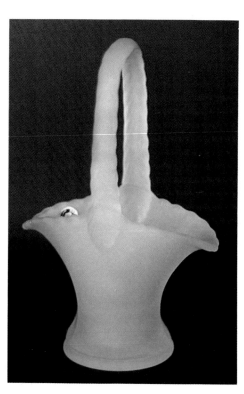

#750. Left: Black shiny with light cutting, 6½", $45.00 – 65.00; right: brown mist satin, 6½", 1970s – 1980s, $20.00 – 30.00.

#750, blue mist satin, 7", 1970s – 1980s, $20.00 – 30.00.

#750. Left: Cobalt carnival, 6½", $20.00 – 30.00; right: ruby with hand painting signed "D. Green 1976," 6¼", $25.00 – 35.00.

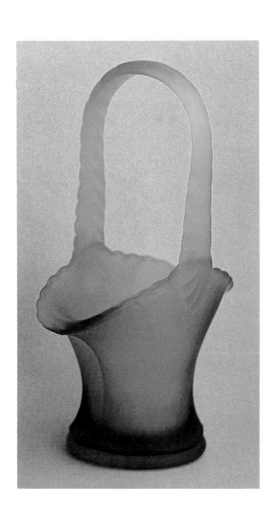

#750, green mist satin, 6½", 1970s – 1980s, $20.00 – 30.00.

#750. Left: Amber, 6½", "WG" molded in base, $15.00 – 25.00; right: blue, 6", "WG" molded in base, $20.00 – 30.00.

#755, green, 11½", $85.00 – 125.00.

#755, clear with light cutting, 10¼", $55.00 – 75.00.

#752, clear with acid etched basket of flowers in medallion, 9", $40.00 – 50.00.

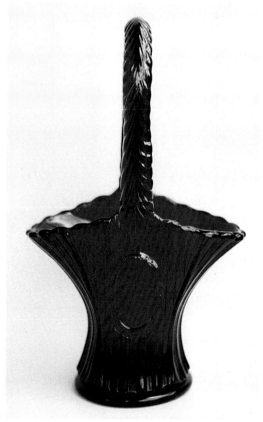

#752, ruby, 10½", $45.00 – 65.00.

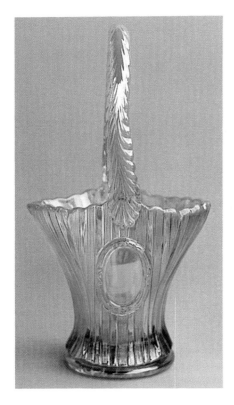

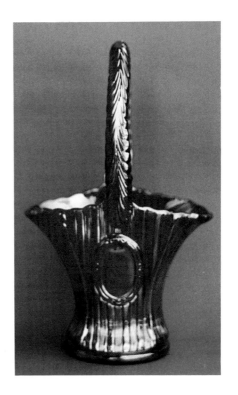

#752, green carnival, 10½", $40.00 –
55.00.

#752, red carnival, 10½", $40.00 –
55.00.

Left: English
Hobnail in
cobalt, 9", newer,
rim not flared
out, "Westmore-
land W" molded
in base, $85.00 –
125.00.

Right: English
Hobnail in milk
(opal), 9", newer,
rim not flared
out, $10.00 –
20.00.

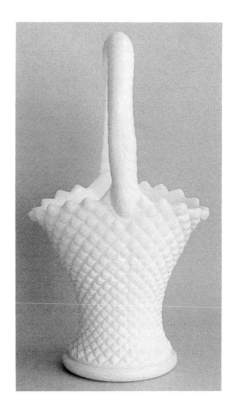

English Hobnail. Left: Amber, 8½", newer, rim not flared out, "Westmoreland W" molded in base, $20.00 – 35.00; right: green carnival, 8¾", newer, rim not flared out, $50.00 – 75.00.

English Hobnail. Left: Blue, 9¼", label "Westmoreland Glass," $85.00 – 125.00; right: ruby, 9½", $85.00 – 125.00.

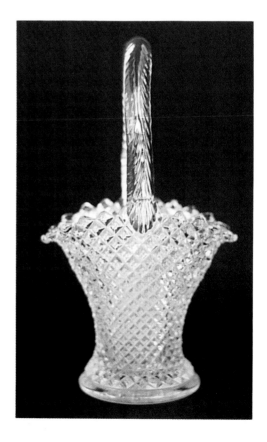

Left: English Hobnail in amber, 9½", a good example of the older style with the rim flared out and down, $35.00 – 55.00.

Right: English Hobnail in clear, 9", $20.00 – 30.00.

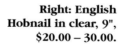

#757, Pansy.
Left: Amber, 4",
$10.00 – 15.00;
right: gold
flashing, 4",
$25.00 – 35.00.

#757, Pansy. Left: Clear with ruby and lavender flashing, 3½", $25.00 – 35.00; right: green, 3½", label with "Westmoreland Handmade Glass," $10.00 – 15.00.

Swirl & Ball. Left:
Amber, 3½", $10.00
– 15.00; right: clear
with ruby and
lavender flashing,
3½", $25.00 –
35.00.

#757, Pansy in blue milk, 3½", $15.00 – 25.00.

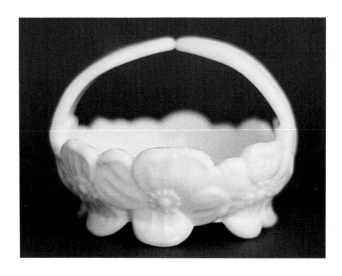

#757, Pansy in milk (opal), 3½", $10.00 – 15.00.

Woolworth, in pink, 4", $20.00 – 35.00.

Paneled Grape in clear with ruby flashed grapes, 4", $30.00 – 45.00.

Paneled Grape in milk (opal), 4", molded "WMG" in base, $10.00 – 20.00.

Hen on nest, 4¾", $50.00 – 75.00.

Log cabin in amber, 5", label with "Westmoreland Glass," $10.00 – 25.00.

Blue mist with Mary Gregory decoration, 7", $100.00 – 150.00.

L.G. Wright • New Martinsville, West Virginia
1960s – 1999

Daisy & Button. Left: Amethyst, 7½", $40.00 – 50.00; right: amber, 7½", $25.00 – 35.00.

Daisy & Button. Left: Yellow vaseline, 7½", $65.00 – 75.00; right: blue, 7½", $45.00 – 55.00.

Imported Glass Baskets

England

Pressed with loop handle, 7", "#R438052" molded on outer edge, $25.00 – 45.00.

China

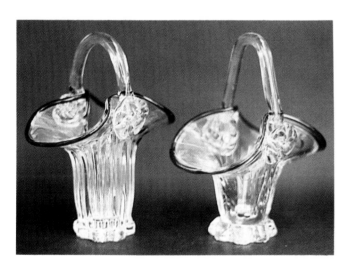

(Above) Left: Clear with cobalt rim, 6¾", label "Gorgeous Designs, China"; right: clear with cobalt rim, 6", $10.00 – 18.00 each.

(Right) Clear with black handle and base and green rim, 6½", $15.00 – 25.00.

Imported Glass Baskets

Czechoslovakia/Bohemia

Prior to 1918, Bohemia existed as a part of the Austro-Hungarian Empire and made some of the most beautiful glass in the history of the world. At the end of World War I, Bohemia became the western part of the new nation of Czecho-Slovakia, and continued to produce wonderful glassware. Thus, anything marked with a variation of the name Czechoslovakia was made after 1918.

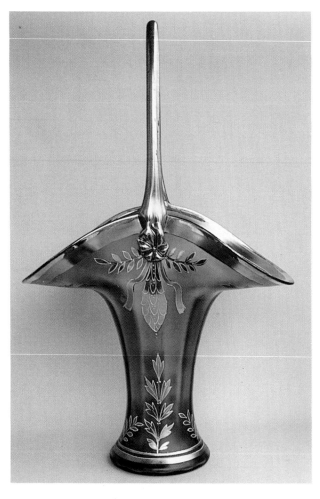

Green with gold enameling, 15", attributed to Bohemia, $450.00 – 550.00.

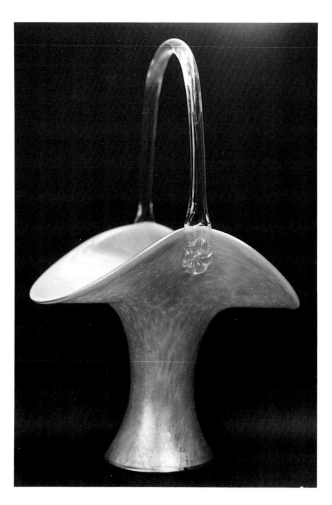

Cased iridescent mottled stretch, 16", attributed to Bohemia, $450.00 – 550.00.

Purple swirl cased, 12½", "Czechoslovakia" etched in bottom, $250.00 – 350.00.

Red with black enamel, 10½", unmarked, $250.00 – 350.00.

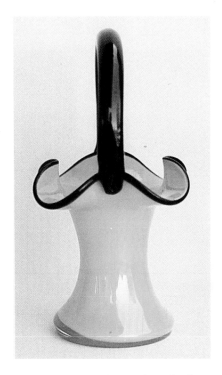

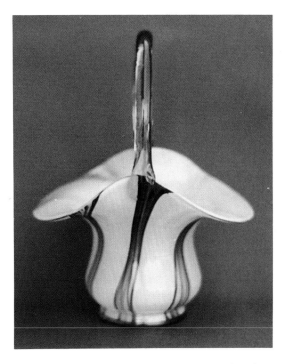

Yellow and black cased with clear, 6¾", "Czechoslovakia" etched in base, $85.00 – 150.00.

Carmel and cream cased, 9", "Czechoslovakia" etched in base, $75.00 – 150.00.

Multicolored swirl, "Czechoslovakia" etched in base, $75.00 – 150.00.

Spatter or confetti (This type of glass is often called "End of Day," but considering the amount of it that has been made over the last 125 years or so, glassmakers' days must have been endless!), 6", "Czechoslovakia" etched in base, $75.00 – 150.00.

Spatter/confetti/end of day, 6", "Czechoslovakia" etched in base, $75.00 – 150.00.

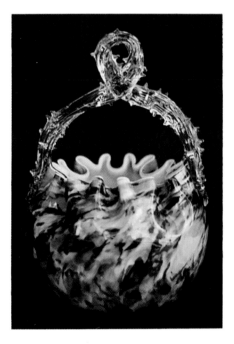

Early twentieth century Bohemian spatter/confetti/end of day, 7", unmarked, $75.00 – 150.00.

Spatter/confetti/end of day, 6", "Czechoslovakia" etched in base, $75.00 – 150.00.

Spatter/confetti/end of day, 7½", $75.00 – 150.00.

Ruby with gold and multicolored enamel decoration. Left: 9", label "Bohemian Crystal Made in Czechoslovakia," circa 1988; right: 6½", label "Genuine Hand Decorated RTL Made in Czechoslovakia," circa 1973, $85.00 – 150.00 each.

Ruby with gold and multicolored enamel decoration, unmarked. Left: 8½", circa 1972; right: 8", circa 1989, $85.00 – 150.00 each.

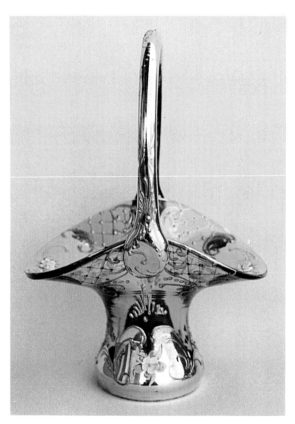

Blue with gold and multicolored enamel decoration, unmarked, 7", circa 1985, $85.00 – 150.00.

Ruby cut to clear, 8½", label "Bohemia Crystal Made in Czechoslovakia," $45.00 – 85.00.

Left: Cobalt with gold and multicolored enamel decoration, 4½"; right: milk (opal) cased with pink with gold and multicolored enamel decoration, 4¾", $65.00 – 75.00 each.

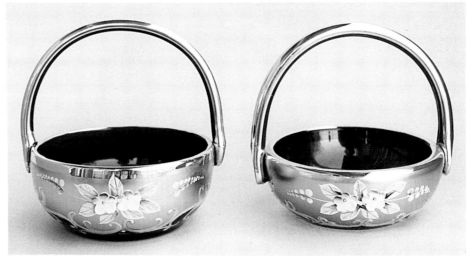

Left: Cobalt with gold and multicolored enamel decoration, 4½"; right: ruby with gold and multicolored enamel decoration, 4½"; both with label "Genuine Hand Decorated RTL Made in Czechoslovakia," $65.00 – 75.00 each.

Green with clear rigaree (the decorative ring around the bowl of the basket) handle and foot, 9", marked "Czechoslovakia," $35.00 – 55.00.

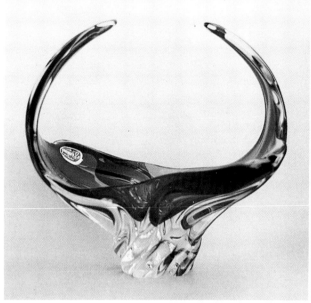

(Left) Cobalt cased with clear split handle, 4¾", label "Chřibska Czech Republic," $30.00 – 45.00.

(Above) Ruby cased with clear split handle, 9½", label "Bohemia Glass Made in Czech Republic," $40.00 – 60.00.

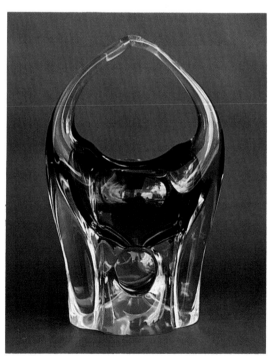

Ruby cased with clear split handle, 9¾", label "Glassworks Chřibska Czech Republic," $40.00 – 60.00.

Ruby cased with clear split handle, 7½," label "Bohemia Glass Made in Czechoslovakia," $35.00 – 45.00.

Germany

Clear with light cutting. Left: 6", label "German Lead Crystal," circa 1972; right: 6½", unmarked, $50.00 – 75.00 each.

Clear with cutting, 8½", unmarked, $50.00 – 75.00.

Clear with cutting, 8¼", label "Genuine Lead Crystal Over 24% Lead Oxide Hand Cut Made in West Germany," $50.00 – 75.00.

Byrde's basket, clear with gold flashing, 7", label "Hofbauer Made in Germany," $60.00 – 95.00.

Byrde's basket, clear with ruby flashing, 10½", label "Hofbauer Made in Germany," $60.00 – 95.00.

Byrde's basket, clear, 7", label "Hoffbauer Collection Made in Germany Over 24.5% Leaded Crystal," $60.00 – $95.00.

Byrde's basket with triple handle, 6¾", label unreadable, $80.00 – 125.00.

Pressed with light cutting, 6", label "Crystal Clear Made in West Germany," $25.00 – 45.00.

Cut to clear. Left: Green, 5½", unmarked; right: cobalt, unmarked, 5", $45.00 – 55.00 each.

Cobalt cut to clear, 7", label "Made in German Democratic Republic, Crystal Glass Industries," $55.00 – $75.00.

Italy

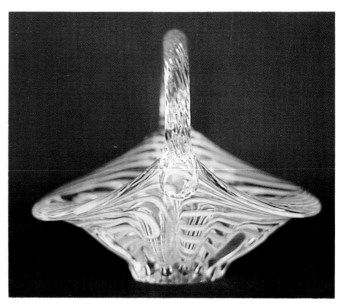

Milk (opal) cased with yellow, 9½", $85.00 – 125.00.

Clear threaded with green, 6¼", unmarked, Murano style, attributed to Italy, $40.00 – 70.00.

Lavender with mica flecks, 7", unmarked, attributed to Italy, $45.00 – 60.00.

Lavender with mica flecks, 7", unmarked, attributed to Italy, $85.00 – 100.00.

Left: Ribbon striped, 10", circa 1972, $75.00 – 125.00; right: millefiori, 8½", label "Made in Murano Italy," circa 1987, $75.00 – 125.00.

Millefiori, 5", unmarked, attributed to Italy, circa 1979, $70.00 – 90.00.

Millefiori, 7½", unmarked, attributed to Italy, circa 1973, $55.00 – 75.00.

Blue swirl, 9¾", circa 1971, marked "Italy," $20.00 – 30.00.

Amber lattice, 9½", marked "Italy," $85.00 – 125.00.

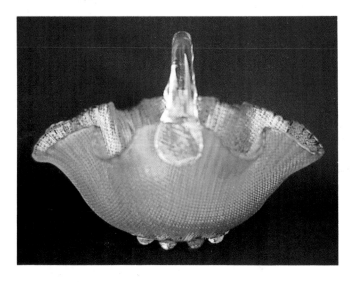

Criss-cross or "burlap" texture, 6¼", unmarked, attributed to Italy because of other marked pieces in the same "burlap" style, $25.00 – 45.00.

Venetian or Murano style spatter/confetti/end of day, attributed to Italy, 4¾", $35.00 – 45.00.

Romania

Left: Cobalt with clear, 7½"; right: spatter/confetti/end of day, 7½"; $15.00 – 20.00 each.

Taiwan

Basketweaves. Left: Satin; right: clear, 1½" to 3½", $3.00 – 5.00 each.

Spun glass with glass fruits, 2" – 3¼", $12.00 – 18.00 each.

Miscellaneous Glass Baskets

American & Imported

Left: Knockoff of Heisey's Double Rib Panel, 8", $45.00 – 65.00. (See page 52.)

Right: Clear with amber handle and base and cutting, 6½", $165.00 – 175.00. (See Libby ad at the end of this book.)

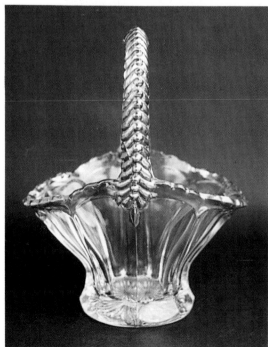

Colonial style six panels, 30 uneven rays similar to Tiffin #9581, but with a smooth rim and handle, 7½", $30.00 – 45.00. (See page 80.)

Paneled clear with gold flashing, 6¼", $20.00 – 30.00.

San Francisco souvenir similar to Duncan and Westmoreland's #750, but with prominent mold seams under the handle, 6", $25.00 – 35.00. (See pages 19 and 86.)

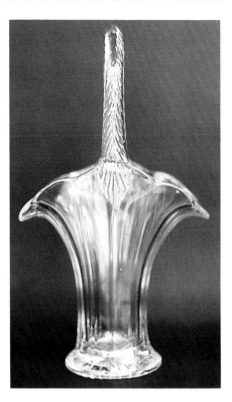

Colonial 12 panels, 24 rays, 12", $65.00 – 85.00.

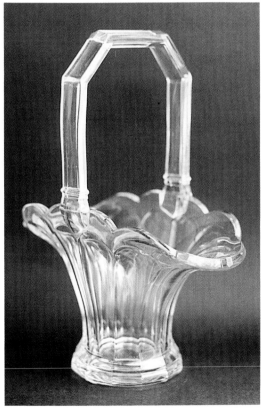

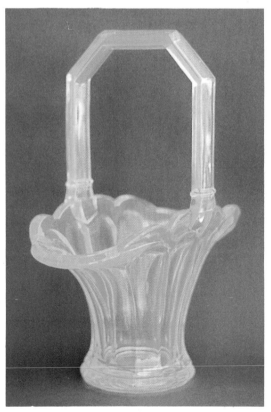

Colonial with Heisey look-alike angled handle, 9½", $60.00 – 80.00.

Colonial with Heisey look-alike angled handle in yellow vaseline, 10", $95.00 – 115.00.

Miscellaneous Glass Baskets

"Pittsburgh 1919" souvenir, 6", $25.00 – 35.00.

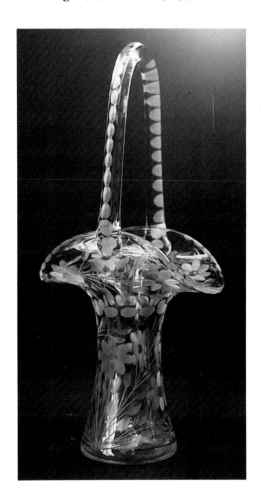

Colonial 12 panel, 20 rays, 8", $30.00
– 45.00.

Clear with light cutting, 14", $200.00 – 225.00.

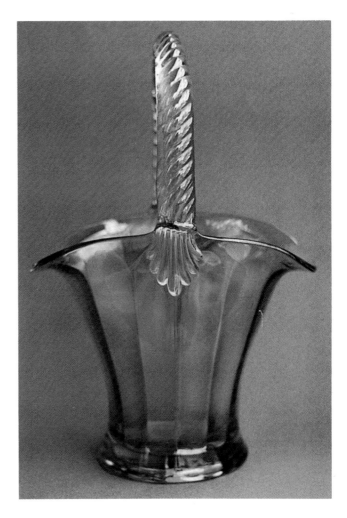

Colonial in marigold carnival, eight panels, 10½",
$70.00 – 90.00.

Colonial in marigold carnival, 12 panels, no rays, 9½",
$70.00 – 90.00.

Miscellaneous Glass Baskets

Left: Green with gold and multicolored enamel decoration, 5¾"; right: blue with gold and multicolored enamel decoration, 6½", $50.00 – 60.00 each.

Pink with black enamel decoration, 13", $65.00 – 85.00.

Left: Ruby with clear, 7¼"; right: yellow with clear, 4½", $30.00 – 45.00 each.

Blue with floral decals, 6¼", $45.00 – 60.00.

Iridescent art glass with threading decoration, 6" – 6¾", $125.00 – 165.00 each.

Milk (opal) and blue cased with clear, 8", $35.00 – 55.00.

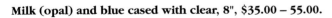

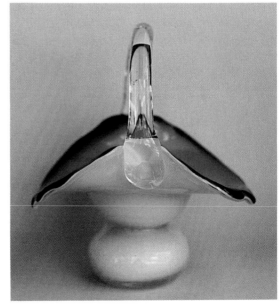

Red and clear satin glass, 6", circa 1970s, $15.00 – 25.00.

Blue cased with milk (opal), 4¼", $20.00 – 25.00.

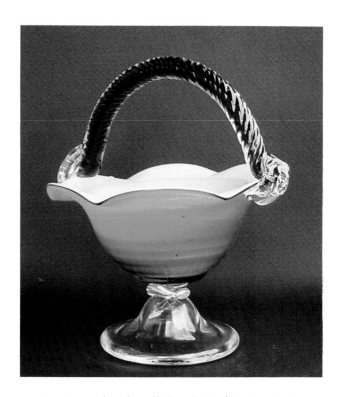

Green cased with milk (opal), 7", $25.00 – 35.00.

Emerald green with silver overlay, 10", $200.00 – 250.00.

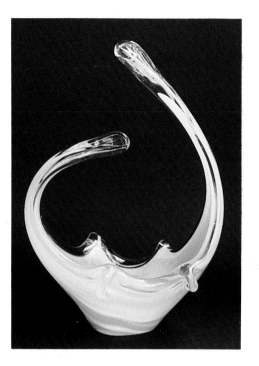

Transluscent pink with crystal crest, foot and rigaree, 10¼", $50.00 – 75.00.

Green and white slag split handle, 9", $20.00 – 35.00.

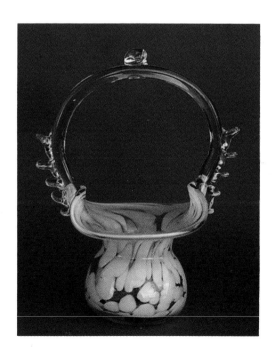

Spatter/confetti/end of day, 6¾", $15.00 – 20.00.

Milk (opal) and ruby cased with clear, Romanian, 7½", $15.00 – 20.00.

Miscellaneous Glass Baskets

Left: Cobalt 7¼"; right: deep ruby, Romanian, 7", $12.00 – 18.00 each. (Pictured in import catalogs for about $8.00 – 9.00 wholesale.)

Cobalt cased with clear, 7", $12.00 – 18.00.

Victorian & Early 20th Century Art Glass Baskets, American & Imported

This section includes some look-alikes. They are baskets that can appear older than they really are.

Bushel basket toothpick holder in blue opalescent, 3¼", $55.00 – 75.00.

Opalescent blue footed bushel, 2¾", $55.00 – 75.00.

Opalescent with crimped rim, 4¼", $125.00 – 175.00.

Opalescent with twisted handle, 4¾", $85.00 – 125.00.

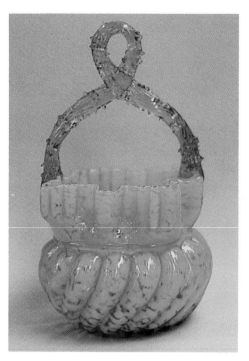

"Look-alike," blue swirl with mica flecks in clear handle, 8", $35.00 – 50.00.

Blue with thorn handle, 8½" circa 1894 – 1896, $300.00 – 350.00.

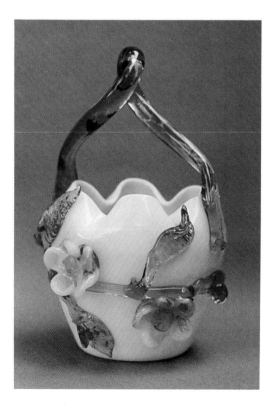

Custard with applied amber handle and flowers, 7", $200.00 – 225.00.

Burmese, 10½", $125.00 – $175.00.

Old Man Winter (so named by William Heacock), Jefferson Glass Co. #135, circa 1906. Left: Green; right, blue; 4½", $75.00 – 125.00 each.

Persimmon cased with ochre and clear, 5¾", $300.00 – 350.00.

Jefferson Glass May basket, blue opalescent, 5½", $75.00 – 125.00.

Jefferson Glass May basket, clear with opalescent handle, 6½", $75.00 – 125.00.

Persimmon cased with ochre and clear, 8", $300.00 – 350.00.

Pink overshot, 9", $225.00 – 250.00.

Clear overshot, 7½", $200.00 – 225.00.

Heat struck pink to yellow with green vaseline handle, 5", $350.00 – 400.00.

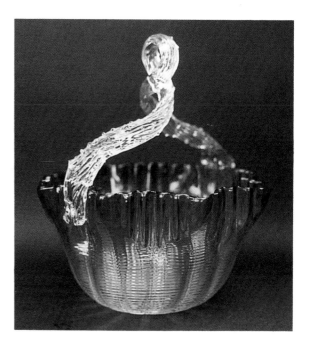

Rubina, similar to Northwood's Jewel or Threaded Swirl, but not swirled, 7½", $450.00 – 500.00.

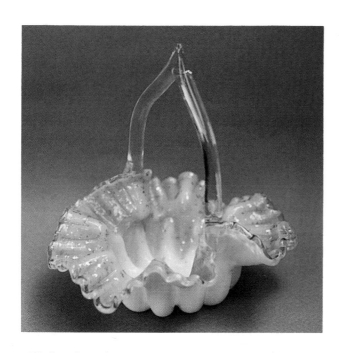

Milk (opal) with tan and mica flecks, 7¼", $300.00 – 350.00.

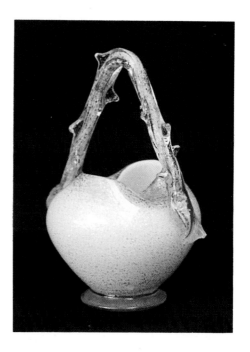

Milk (opal) with pink thorn handle, 5½", may have hung from an armature, $120.00 – 130.00.

French art glass, 9", $450.00 – 500.00.

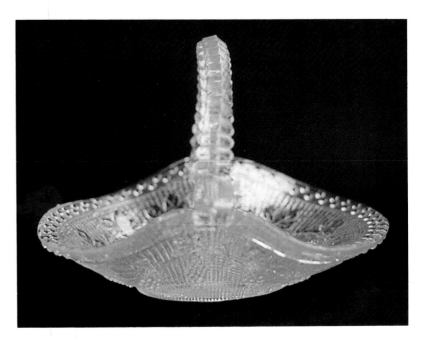

Yellow vaseline with block handle, 5", $90.00 – 110.00.

Amber with block handle, 4¼", $50.00 – 75.00.

Sandwich style with twig handle, 6¼", $50.00 – 75.00.

"Look-alike," amber with three feet and twig handle, 8", $35.00 – 50.00.

"Look-alike," blue with twig handle, 5½", $50.00 – 65.00.

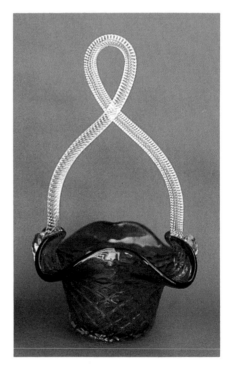

"Look-alike," milk (opal), with label "Hand Blown Toscany Made in China," circa 1986, $8.00 – 15.00.

"Look-alike," ruby with clear handle, 9", label "Handcrafted in Canada, Rieke's Chalet, Lead Crystal," $20.00 – 35.00.

Abingdon Stars, 7¾", $25.00 – 35.00 each.

Bel-Terr China USA, weeping gold, 3", $45.00 – 60.00.

Fulper (Vasekraft), 5", $450.00 – 550.00 each.

Hull Wildflower, W-16, 10½", pink and blue, $350.00 – 375.00.

Hull Water Lily, L-14, 10½", pink and green, $340.00 – 360.00.

Hull Open Rose, 107-8, 8¾", pink and blue, $340.00 – 360.00.

Hull Tulip, 102-38-6, blue and white, 7½", $240.00 – 260.00.

**Hull Tulip, 102-38-6, pink and blue, 7½",
$240.00 – 260.00.**

Hull Iris, 408-7, 7½", pink and blue, $320.00 – 330.00.

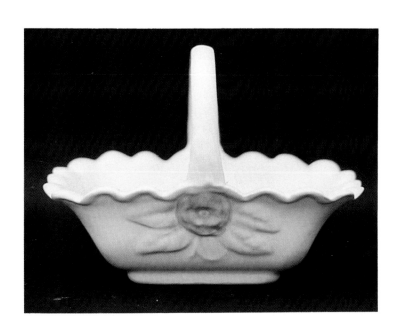

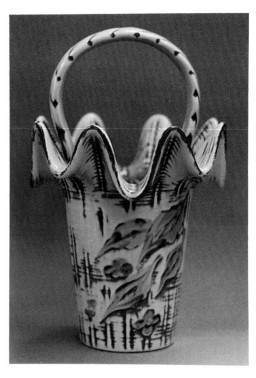

Hull Open Rose, 142, 6¼", in pink and white, $320.00 – 330.00.

Hull Blossom Flight, T4C, 1955, 9", $90.00 – 110.00.

Hull Imperial, 6½", $25.00 – 35.00.

Lenox, marked in gold "Lenox Made in USA," 5½"
$30.00 – 40.00.

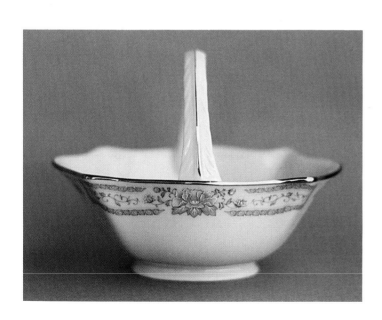

Lenox, Charleston pattern, 4¾", $30.00 – 40.00.

McCoy Leaves and Berries, 8", $35.00 – 55.00.

Pennsbury Bird on Gourd, blue and white, 5", $100.00 – 125.00.

Pennsbury Bird on Gourd, yellow and green, 5", $20.00 – 35.00 each.

Roseville Apple Blossom, 309, 8", 1948, blue, $325.00 – 400.00.

Roseville Bittersweet, 809, 8", 1940, yellow, $225.00 – 300.00.

Roseville Bittersweet, 808, 6", 1940, green, $175.00 – 200.00.

Roseville Blackberry, 7½", 1933, green, $1,000.00 – 1,100.00.

Roseville Bleeding Heart, 10¼", 1938, blue, $550.00 – 650.00.

Roseville Bushberry, 369, 6½", 1941, blue, $250.00 – 325.00.

Roseville Bushberry, 12", 1941, green, $390.00 – 450.00.

Roseville Columbine, 366, 8", 1940, brown, $250.00 – 325.00.

Roseville Cosmos, 10", 1940, green, $350.00 – 425.00.

Roseville Cosmos, 358, 12", 1940, green, $475.00 – 550.00.

**Roseville Dog-
wood II, 9¼",
1928, $325.00 –
375.00.**

**Roseville Dogwood
II, 9", 1928, $350.00 –
400.00.**

**Roseville Dogwood
II, 9¾", 1928,
$325.00 – 375.00.**

Roseville Foxglove, 373, 8", 1940, blue, $275.00 –
300.00.

American Ceramic Baskets

Roseville Imperial I, 7¾", 1916, $225.00 – 275.00.

Roseville Imperial I, 10", 1916, $275.00 – 300.00.

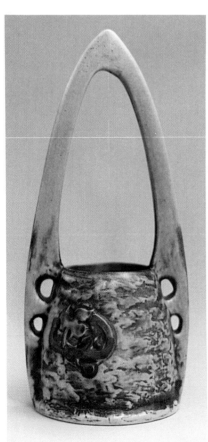

Roseville Imperial I, 12", 1916, $300.00 – 350.00.

Roseville Imperial I, 6", 1916, $225.00 – 275.00.

Roseville Imperial I, with reticulated handle, 5¾", 1916, $265.00 – 300.00.

Roseville Imperial I, 8", 1916, $225.00 – 275.00.

Roseville Iris, 10", 1938, $450.00 – 550.00.

Roseville Jonquil, 1931, 6¾", $400.00 – 500.00.

Roseville Jonquil, 1931, 6", $400.00 – 500.00.

Roseville Mock Orange, 911, 10", 1950, $225.00 – 275.00.

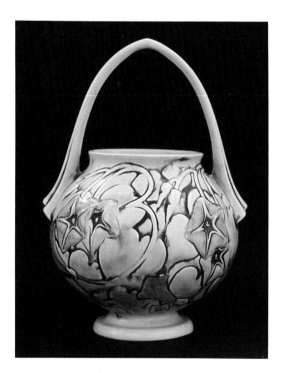

Roseville Monticello, 6¾", 1931, $850.00 – 950.00.

Roseville Morning Glory, 11", 1935, white, $850.00 – 1,000.00.

Roseville Pine Cone, 353, 11", 11½", $700.00 – 750.00.

Roseville Pine Cone, 408, 6", 1931, $300.00 – 375.00.

Roseville Pine Cone, 408, 6", 1931, brown, $425.00 – 500.00.

Roseville Pine Cone, 410, 10", 1931, $500.00 – 550.00.

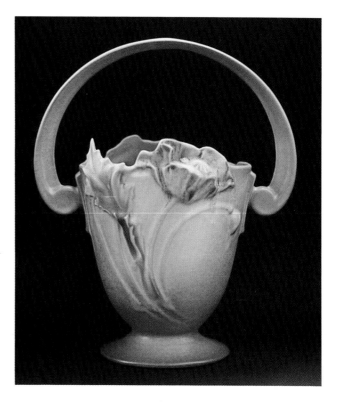

Roseville Pine Cone, 10½", green, $475.00 – 550.00.

Roseville Poppy, 10", 1930, $400.00 – 475.00.

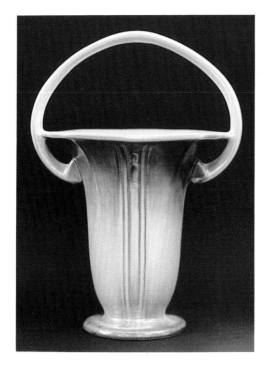

Roseville Russco, 10", early 1930s, $275.00 – 325.00.

Roseville Silhouette, 6¾", 1952, $175.00 – 200.00.

Roseville Thornapple, 10", 1930, $275.00 – 325.00.

Roseville Vista (a.k.a. Forest), 6½", 1920, $950.00 – 1,050.00.

Roseville Vista (a.k.a. Forest), 6¾", 1920, $950.00 – 1,050.00.

Roseville Wincraft, #208, 8½", 1948, $100.00 – 125.00.

American Ceramic Baskets

Weller, 4½", $65.00 – 85.00.

Roseville Zephyr Lily, 393, 7", 1940s, $150.00 – 200.00.

Attributed to Weller, pink lustre, 8", $75.00 – 90.00.

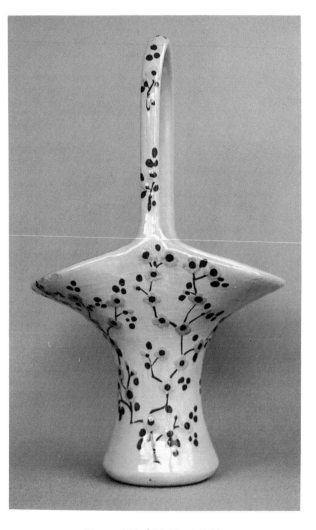

Yona, 12", $50.00 – 75.00.

Imported Ceramic Baskets

China

Imitation of antique Chinese basket, 2½", $25.00 – 40.00.

Easter basket with eggs, 3¾", label "Made in China," $15.00 – 25.00.

Above: Close-up of mark on Satsuma basket at left.

Left: New imitation of Japanese Satsuma, 8", label "Made in China, Satsuma," $50.00 – 75.00.

Calla lily basket, 4¼", label "Handcrafted for © Silvestri Made in China," $5.00 – 8.00.

Lace edge, 2¼", backstamp "China," $5.00 – 7.00.

White with pink flowers, 4", left: marked "Made in China"; right: no mark, $3.00 – 5.00 each.

Trinket box baskets, 2¾", label "Made in China," $5.00 – 7.00 each.

Flat with sprigged-on flowers, 2¾", $25.00 – 35.00.

Czechoslovakia

Multicolored Art Deco, 9", $45.00 – 65.00.

Cream lustre glaze with orange handle, 4", $15.00 – 25.00.

Purse-style, marked "Czechoslovakia." Left: 4½", $20.00 – 35.00; right: 3½", $18.00 – 25.00.

Purse-style, with Asian motif, 4½", marked "Czechoslovakia," $35.00 – 55.00.

Purse-style, marked "Czechoslovakia," 4½", $15.00 – 25.00.

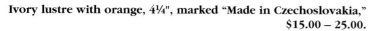

Ivory lustre with orange, 4¼", marked "Made in Czechoslovakia," $15.00 – 25.00.

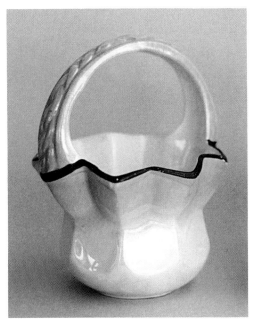

Cream and blue with rose decal, 4¼", marked "Made in Czechoslovakia," $20.00 – 30.00.

Bag-style, 3¾", marked "Made in Czechoslovakia," $15.00 – 25.00.

Ivory lustre with black, 4¾", marked "Made in Czechoslovakia," $15.00 – 25.00.

Yellow lustre with green, 4½", marked "Czechoslovakia," $15.00 – 25.00.

Imported Ceramic Baskets

England

Gold lustre with floral motif, 2½", marked "Wood & Son 1480E, Burselm, England," $35.00 – 55.00.

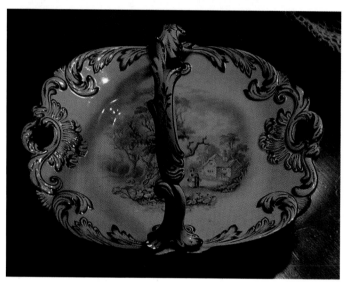

Staffordshire-type transfer ware basket, 6", English, nineteenth century, $650.00 – 850.00.

Chintz, Royal Winton, Sunshine pattern, 5", marked "Made in England," $100.00 – 135.00.

Royal Winton, 5", marked "Made in England," $30.00 – 45.00.

Green with roses, 4", marked "Fine Bone China, Crown Staffordshire, Made in England," $30.00 – 45.00.

"Dolly Varden" style, 4", marked "Jubilee Fine Bone China, Made in England," $15.00 – 25.00.

Green with gold trim, 3¼", marked "England," $15.00 – 25.00.

France

Basket, 3", marked in red "Limoges AK/CD France" and in green "Limoges," in a star, $65.00 – 75.00.

Limoges, 3½", $65.00 – 75.00.

Limoges gold on gold, "Dolly Varden" style, 5", marked "B & Co Tiks Hand Painted, Limoges, France," $65.00 – 85.00.

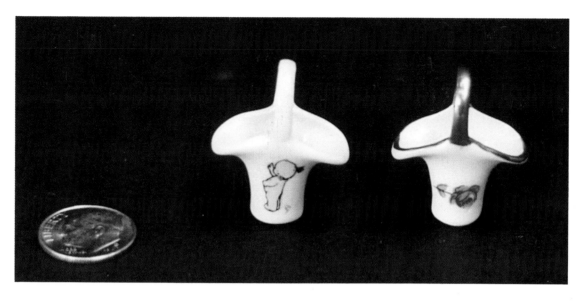

Limoges miniatures, 1½". Left: Kewpie, $45.00 – 65.00; right: rose, $25.00 – 45.00.

Purse-style, 4¾", marked "China T & V France 6302," $25.00 – 35.00.

Germany (Austria, Bavaria, Germany, Prussia, Silesia)

Teplitz, Austria, a variety of Amphora, 3½", $125.00 – 150.00.

Yellow "Dolly Varden" style, 5½", marked "Victoria Austria," $50.00 – 75.00.

Hand painted by Smith, probably painted in the blank, 3¼", marked "Z.S. & CO. Bavaria," $20.00 – 30.00.

Nut cup, 2¾", marked Thames, Bavaria, $25.00 – 35.00.

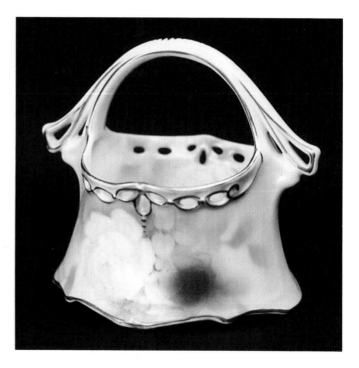

Royal Bayreuth floral style, #388, 4¼", blue mark, $300.00 – 350.00.

Royal Bayreuth rose tapestry, 4", $450.00 – 550.00.

Royal Bayreuth rose tapestry, 5½", $400.00 – 500.00.

Royal Bayreuth "Dolly Varden" style, rose tapestry in yellow, blue mark, 4½", $325.00 – 395.00.

Royal Bayreuth "Dolly Varden" style, rose tapestry in pink, blue mark, 4½", $350.00 – 450.00.

Royal Bayreuth "Dolly Varden" style, tapestry with portrait, green mark, 4½", $600.00 – 650.00.

Schafer & Vater with roses, 4½", $85.00 – 110.00.

Schafer & Vater with roses, 4½", $85.00 – 110.00.

Schafer & Vater with cameo portrait, 6", circa 1910, $200.00 – 225.00.

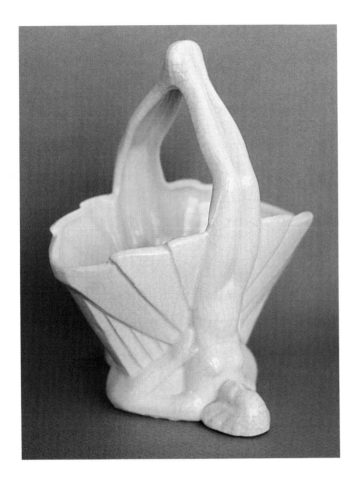

Left: Art Deco with two reclining nudes in cream crackle glaze, 8¾", incised "9221" on base, $45.00 – 75.00.

Above: Blue, 4¾", marked "Jasba, Germany 1900," $15.00 – 25.00.

Left: Silver wash with black handle, 4¼", marked "RS Germany" in blue, $40.00 – 60.00; right: platinum with etched surface, 4", marked "RS Germany" with "J. Hinton Platinum China," $40.00 – 60.00.

Purse-style, with hand-painted roses, 5¾", $25.00 – 45.00.

Fruit-decorated, 5", late 1800s, unmarked, $70.00 – 95.00.

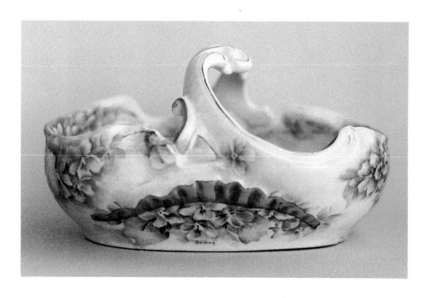

Painted in blank, signed "Ramey," 3½", $30.00 – 45.00.

Twig handle, 5", no mark, $25.00 – 45.00.

Metallic-glazed blossom, "Souvenir of Easton PA," 3¼", $20.00 – 35.00.

Left: Souvenir, "Mt. Hood from Lost Lake," 5", $25.00 – 45.00; right: "Souvenir Stockton Cal." 5", $25.00 – 45.00.

Souvenir, "Chamber of Commerce, Portland Oregon," 5", $25.00 – 45.00.

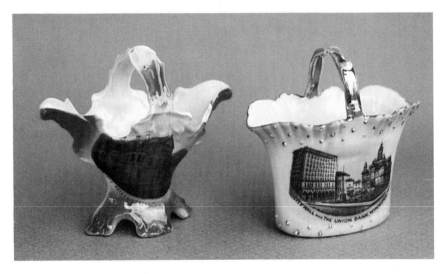

Left: Souvenir, "State Prison, Stillwater Minn.," 3", $25.00 – 45.00; right: souvenir, "City Hall & Union Bank, Winnepeg Manitoba," 3¼", $25.00 – 45.00.

Left: Souvenir, "Court House, Dixon Ill.," 3½", marked "Made in Germany for Leslie Bros Dixon Ill.," $25.00 – 45.00; right: souvenir "Philadelphia Pa.," 3½", marked "Made in Germany," $25.00 – 45.00.

Left: "Souvenir of San Antonio Texas," 4", marked "Made in Germany," $25.00 – 45.00; right: "Souvenir of Red Oak Iowa," 3½", $25.00 – 45.00.

Souvenir, "County Courthouse Tacoma Wash," 4¼", $25.00 – 45.00.

Gold lustre glaze with portrait, 5", $15.00 – 25.00.

Left to right: White lustre glaze with embossed cherries, 4"; white lustre glaze with red flower, 3¾"; gold lustre glaze with pansy, 3", $15.00 – 25.00 each.

Lattice weave with sprigged-on flowers and leaves, 3½", marked "Germany," $20.00 – 35.00.

Left: Nut cup with sprigged-on flowers, 4", marked "Germany," $15.00 – 25.00; right: blue basketweave salt dip, 2", marked "Germany," $15.00 – 25.00.

Nut cups. Left to right: 1¾", marked "Germany"; 2", marked "Germany"; 2¼", unmarked; 1¾", marked "Germany,"
$15.00 – 25.00 each.

Left to right: Nut cup, marked "Germany," 2¾"; favor vase, no mark, 2½"; salt dip, no mark, 1¼"; nut cup, marked
"Germany," 1¼", $15.00 – 25.00 each.

Nut cups, marked "Germany," 2", $15.00 – 25.00 each.

Left to right: Salt dip, tan lustre glaze, 1¾", marked "Germany," $15.00 – 25.00; Asian unmarked nutcup "look-alike," 2¾", $3.00 – 8.00; nutcup, white lustre glaze, 2½", marked "Germany," $15.00 – 25.00.

Souvenir of Butchart Gardens, 5", circa 1973, marked "Made in Germany," $10.00 – 20.00.

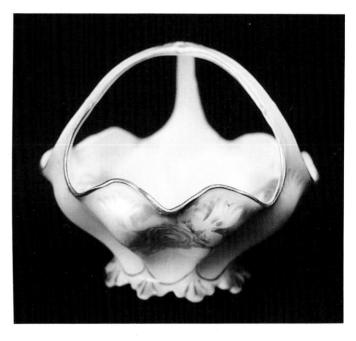

R.S. Prussia with three handles, 5", $450.00 – 550.00.

White glaze with gold leaves, marked "Prussia," 4½", $85.00 – 100.00.

Candy basket painted in blank by Molgel, 3", marked "Silesia" with Crown Mark K S E in blue, $45.00 – 65.00.

Ireland

Left: Belleek open salt with shamrocks, 2½", green mark, 1957 – 1968, $60.00 – 80.00; right: Belleek open salt, 1½", green mark, 1957 – 1968, $40.00 – 50.00.

Italy

Tall "Dolly Varden" style with sprigged-on roses, 9¼", $55.00 – 75.00.

Capodimonte, 3¼", marked with "Crown N," $20.00 – 30.00.

Capodimonte. Left to right: 4½", marked with "Crown N"; 3½", marked with "Crown N"; 4¾", label "Ceramiche e Porcellane N Stilart Capodimonte Made in Italy," $20.00 – 30.00 each.

"Dolly Varden" style with braided handle, 8", $10.00 – 18.00.

Lattice, 3", marked "Italy," $12.00 – 18.00.

Lattice, 3¼", $12.00 – 18.00.

Flat with sprigged-on water lillies, 3", $15.00 – 25.00.

Blue and white pottery with twisted handle, 3¼",
$8.00 – 15.00.

Mottled glaze with leaf, 8", marked "Italy," $5.00 – 8.00.

Dark brown stain, 6½", marked "Made in Italy,"
$5.00 – 8.00.

"Dolly Varden" style with mottled red and green glaze, 3",
marked "Italy," $8.00 – 12.00.

Left: "Dolly Varden" style with bird folk art motif, 3¾", $12.00 – 18.00; right: gray with mottled glaze, 3¾", $8.00 – 12.00.

Japan

Moon vase baskets. Left: Twentieth century Satsuma, 4¾", $125.00 – 150.00; right: late twentieth century, 4¼", marked "HSK Seattle USA Made in Japan," $20.00 – 30.00.

Bucket-style very early twentieth century Satsuma, 3¼", $300.00 – 350.00.

Blue and white glazed bucket-style, 4", $85.00 – 125.00.

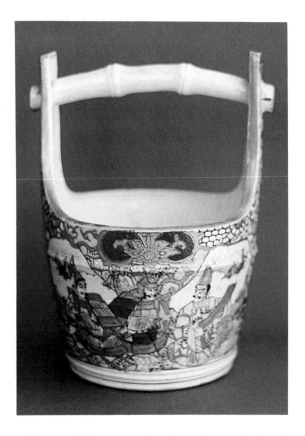

Meiji period, late 1800s, bucket-style, marked with Japanese characters, $300.00 – 375.00.

Mid-twentieth century Satsuma, 7½", $85.00 – 100.00.

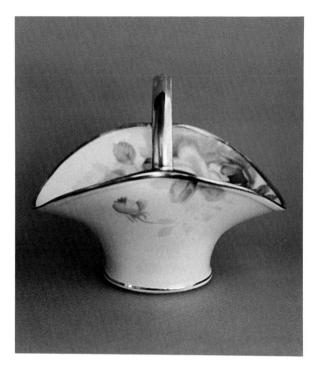

"Dolly Varden" style, 6", marked "Hand Painted Nippon," $45.00 – 65.00.

Flower-shaped, 3", marked "Hand Painted Nippon," $45.00 – 65.00.

Hand-painted Nippon mint baskets. Left: Green with yellow, 2½"; right: blue with blue flowers, $45.00 – 65.00 each.

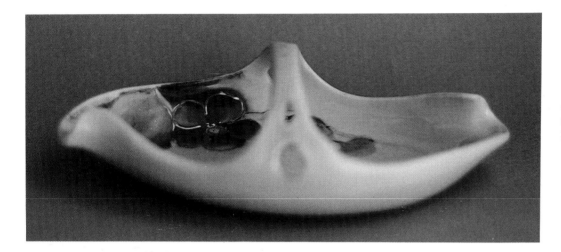

Candy basket, 2",
marked "Hand
Painted Nippon,"
$45.00 – 55.00.

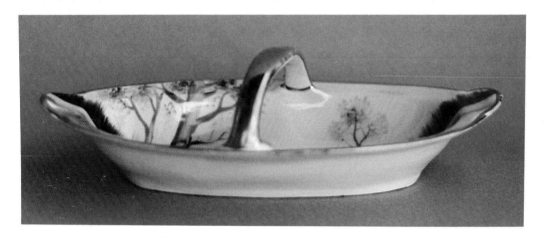

Scenic candy basket,
2½", marked "Hand
Painted Nippon,"
$50.00 – 65.00.

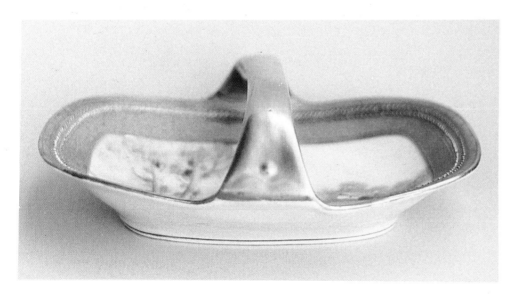

Candy basket, 3", marked
"Hand Painted Nippon,"
$45.00 – 65.00.

Ruffled rim with blue flowers, 5½", marked with red Noritake M in Wreath logo, $40.00 – 55.00.

Tall "Dolly Varden" style, 8", marked with red Noritake M in Wreath logo, $45.00 – 65.00.

Candy basket, 2½", marked with red Noritake M in Wreath logo, $45.00 – 60.00.

Sugar basket with tan lustre glaze and house motif, 4",
marked with red M in Wreath logo, $60.00 – 75.00.

Sugar basket with blue lustre glaze and house motif, 4",
marked with red M in Wreath logo, $60.00 – 75.00.

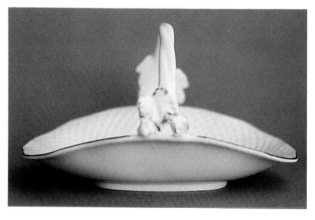

Candy basket with mottled blue glaze, 3", marked "Hand
Painted Made in Japan," $20.00 – 40.00.

Lenox-style glazed basket, 4", marked "Ivory Bone
China, Mikasa, Naruma, Japan," $20.00 – 35.00.

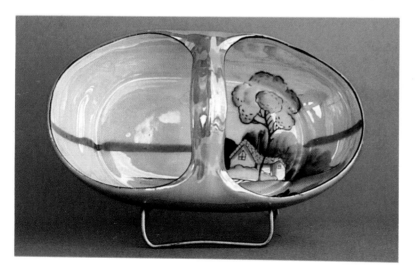

Candy basket with tan lustre glaze and
house motif, 7" wide, $20.00 – 40.00.

Tall "Dolly Varden" style with sprigged-on bird, 6½", $15.00 – 25.00.

Beer stein style motif, 5¼", $15.00 – 25.00.

Boat shape with twig handles, 4", marked "Made in Japan," $15.00 – 25.00.

Rustic style, 3¼", marked "Made in Japan," $8.00 – 15.00.

Basket with daisies, 3¼", marked "Lefton TM Exclusives Japan," $5.00 – 10.00.

Folk art style, 3", marked "Made in Japan," $8.00 – 15.00.

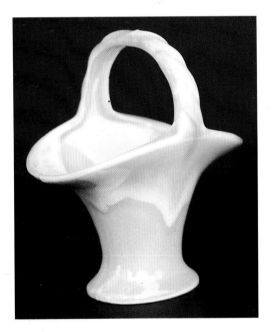

"Dolly Varden" style in yellow drip glaze, 5¼", marked "Made in Japan," $12.00 – 18.00.

"Dolly Varden" style in red drip glaze, 3¾", marked "Made in Japan," $8.00 – 12.00.

Souvenir, "Aloha Hawaii," 4¼", unmarked, $10.00 – 15.00.

White glaze with sprigged-on violets, 4¼", "Made in Japan" blue oval label, $8.00 – 15.00.

Nut cup, 1¾", marked "Made in Occupied Japan," $12.00 – 18.00.

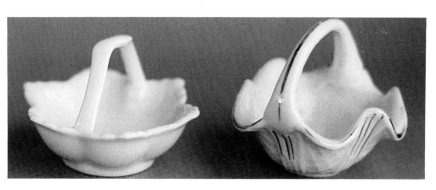

Lace edge, 2½", marked "Made in Japan," $5.00 – 10.00.

Nut cups. Left: 2", marked "Japan"; right: 2¼", marked "Japan," $5.00 – 10.00 each.

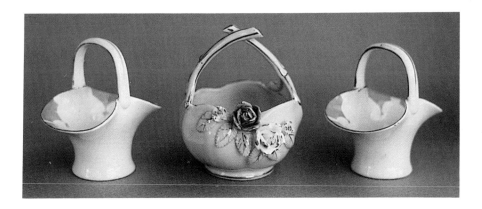

Nut cups. Left and right: 3", marked "Goldcastle Made in Japan"; center: pink with twig handle, marked "Norcrest," $12.00 – 18.00 each.

Nut cup with animal handle, 1½", marked "Made in Japan," $12.00 – 18.00.

Imported Ceramic Baskets • Japan

Left and center: "Dolly Varden" style miniatures, gold and gold with portrait decal, 2", marked "Made in Japan"; right: nut cup, 2½", marked "Made in Japan," $12.00 – 18.00 each.

Noritake "Dolly Varden" style nut cups, 2¼", $30.00 – 40.00 each.

(Above) Left to right: Nut cup, 1½", marked "Made in Japan"; nut cup, 1½", marked "Made in Occupied Japan"; miniature pink "Dolly Varden" style, 2", marked "Made in Occupied Japan"; nut cup, 2", marked "Made in Japan"; $12.00 – 18.00 each.

(Right) Bucket style, 6½", marked "Made in Japan," $15.00 – 25.00.

Nut cups. Left to right: 2¼", marked "Made in Japan"; 2", marked "Japan"; 1¾", no mark; 2", marked "Japan," $12.00 – 18.00 each.

Portugal

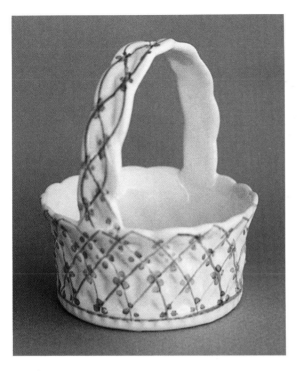

Pink flowers, 5⅛", marked "Hand Painted Portugal RC12 794," $15.00 – 25.00.

Folk art style blue and white, 5", marked "Made in Portugal," $10.00 – 15.00.

Hand painted with double handle, 6½", marked "Portugal," $10.00 – 15.00.

Folk art style blue and white, 5½", label "Made in Portugal Jay Willfred Div. of Andrea by Sadek," $25.00 – 35.00.

Imported Ceramic Baskets

Spain

Woven "Dolly Varden" style, 2½", marked "Levante Made in Spain," $20.00 – 30.00.

Taiwan

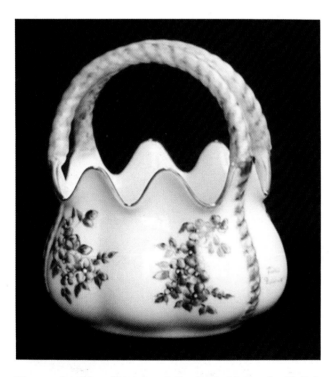

Blue and white, 4", painted for Ruth McCue by T. Fellows, marked "Maryland China Co. Taiwan," $18.00 – 25.00 as painted (unpainted blank $5.00).

"Dolly Varden" style, 5", marked "Taiwan," $5.00 – $10.00.

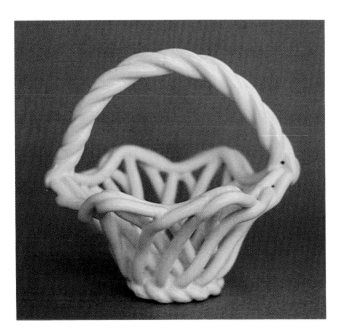

Woven style, 4½", label "PR Maidin Taiwan BBC," $5.00 – 10.00.

Lamb with Easter egg, 3", marked "Enesco Designed Giftware © 1984 Made in Taiwan," $6.00 – 12.00.

White glazed, 5¼", marked "Maryland China Taiwan," $5.00 – 10.00 each.

Imported Ceramic Baskets

Thailand

Nut cups, 1¼" – 3¼", all marked "Thailand," $3.00 – 5.00 each.

Nut cup, 3¼", marked "Made in Thailand," $3.00 – 5.00.

Ceramic "straw" baskets, 1¾" – 2½", all marked "Thailand," $5.00 – 10.00 each.

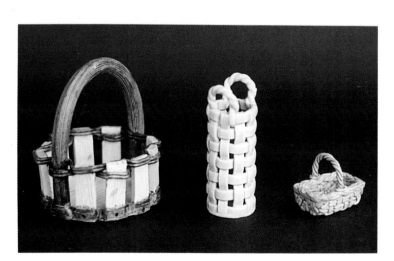

Ceramic "straw" baskets, 1" – 2¾", all marked "Thailand," $5.00 – 10.00 each.

Miscellaneous Ceramic Baskets

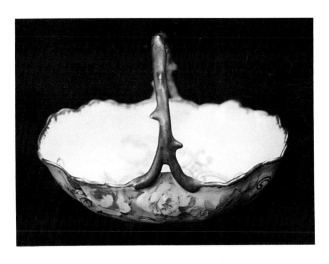

Circa 1890s with thorn handle, 5½", possibly American Belleek, $350.00 – 375.00.

Pottery basketweaves. Left: Blue, 3"; right: green, 3", incised "USA," $12.00 – 22.00 each.

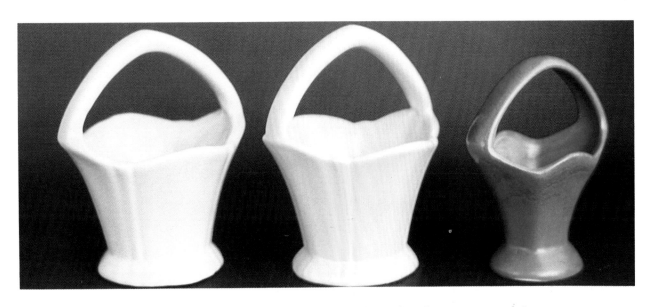

Footed pottery baskets, aqua, yellow, blue, 4¼" – 4½", $15.00 – 22.00 each.

Yellow with sprigged-on rose, 7½", $40.00 – 50.00.

Tall "Dolly Varden" style with grapes, note similarity to Imperial's #714 on page 59, 9½", $20.00 – 35.00.

Tall "Dolly Varden" style with rose decals, 5", no mark, $10.00 – 20.00.

Tall "Dolly Varden" style, folk art style, 7¼", $15.00 – 20.00.

**Crisscross handles with sprigged-on flow-
ers, 4", $20.00 – 25.00.**

**Florida orange, 2¼", the sugar from
a child's dish set, $10.00 – 20.00.**

Chintz, 3½", $35.00 – 60.00.

Smiling pig, 3½", $8.00 – 15.00.

What Is Dolly Varden?

Some of the ceramic baskets in this book are called Dolly Varden. Dolly Varden began life as a character in the novel *Barnaby Rudge* by Charles Dickens, a weekly serial novel published from February 1841 through November 1841. She evidently caught the public's fancy.

In 1883, a woman named Dolly Varden joined Buffalo Bill Cody's Wild West Show. In 1903, a very popular musical comedy called "Dolly Varden" debuted on the Broadway stage. The name was given to a trout, was used on several products such as chololates and spices, and there were dolls sold as Dolly Vardens as well.

The Dolly Varden character was known for her brightly colored dresses, and she is often illustrated holding a basket.

The Noritake China Company called one of its basket shapes the "Dolly Varden" and advertised it as such. This shape, the true Dolly Varden, can be seen on page 152.

It's such a handy name to use that we've borrowed it to describe similar types of baskets.

Following are a couple of period illustrations showing the Dolly Varden character. The basket shown in the picture on page 185 is nothing at all like the Noritake basket shape, so we theorize that they adapted the name due to its popularity, rather than strict adherence to basket type!

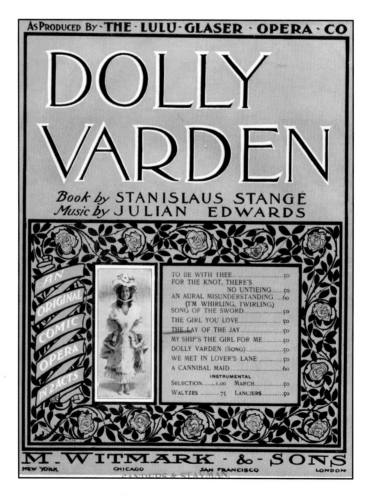

Dolly Varden advertisement.

Dolly Varden advertisement.

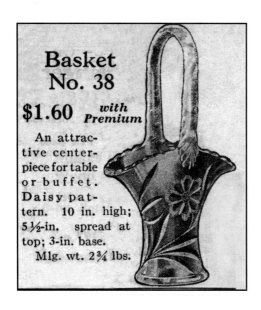

Basket No. 38

$1.60 *with Premium*

An attractive centerpiece for table or buffet. Daisy pattern. 10 in. high; 5 ½-in. spread at top; 3-in. base. Mlg. wt. 2 ¾ lbs.

A reproduction of one of the rare glass treatments of the 19th century, handmade in fine Fenton tradition. Each delicately hand-painted piece is personalized by the artist's signature.

THE FENTON ART GLASS COMPANY, WILLIAMSTOWN, W. VA. 28187

An American Tradition

Considered the finest Milk Glass made, each piece of Fenton hobnail is skillfully handcrafted. Add this extra touch of authentic Early American charm to your home.

Fenton
The Fenton Art Glass Company
Williamstown, West Virginia 26187

Handmade in the fine old Fenton Tradition

FOR A COLORFULLY ILLUSTRATED BOOKLET ABOUT FENTON, ITS ART AND HISTORY 1906-1970, SEND $1

Fenton

ALL THIS —

Appetizers—Arrange Shredded Ralston and cubes of ready-to-eat sausage alternately on toothpicks, topping each one with a pickled onion. Delicious appetizers.

Party Pick-Up—Melt ½ cup butter in skillet. Add pkg. Shredded Ralston. Sprinkle with 1½ tsp. salt. Stir while heating 5 minutes. Serve as nuts, croutons in soup or with fruit juice.

Sugarless Candy—Sweet-tooth thrill for young and old. Easy. Thrifty. Wholesome.

Just do this: Put 2 cups Shredded Ralston in pan over medium heat. Cover with mixture of ¼ cup strained honey and 1 tsp. grated lemon or orange rind. Fold over gently until glazed—about 3 minutes.

AND BREAKFAST, TOO!

IT'S BITE SIZE

Yes...and *what* a breakfast! One look and eyes brighten. One taste and smiles appear. Here's nourishing whole wheat in crisp, tempting bite size form—with an unforgettable flavor. A cereal so just-right in taste, size and crispness it comes in handy from morning to night. Thrifty, too! Costs less per ounce than most nationally advertised ready-to-eat cereals, only half as much as some. Enjoy Shredded Ralston regularly. Remember Uncle Sam says— eat whole grains every day!

BITE SIZE

READY TO EAT

Shredded Ralston

Traditional
Fashions
in Glass

...hand-fashioned by Fenton

Bright-as-spring gifts you'll want for yourself.

The sparkling, gem-like beauty of authentic Fenton Glass is as
welcome as spring itself . . . These exquisitely colored pieces
bring the sunny cheer of the season right into your home! . . .
Indulge your love for lovely things—look for displays of Fenton
handcrafted glassware at fine stores and gift shops everywhere.*

*For names of nearby dealers, write
The Fenton Art Glass Company
Williamstown, West Virginia

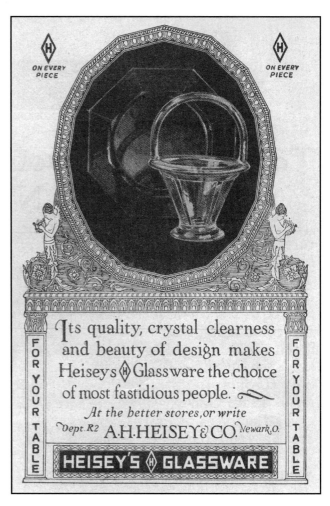

ON EVERY
PIECE   ON EVERY
PIECE

FOR YOUR TABLE

Its quality, crystal clearness
and beauty of design makes
Heisey's Ⓗ Glassware the choice
of most fastidious people.
At the better stores, or write
Dept. R2 A.H. HEISEY & CO. Newark, O.

FOR YOUR TABLE

HEISEY'S Ⓗ GLASSWARE

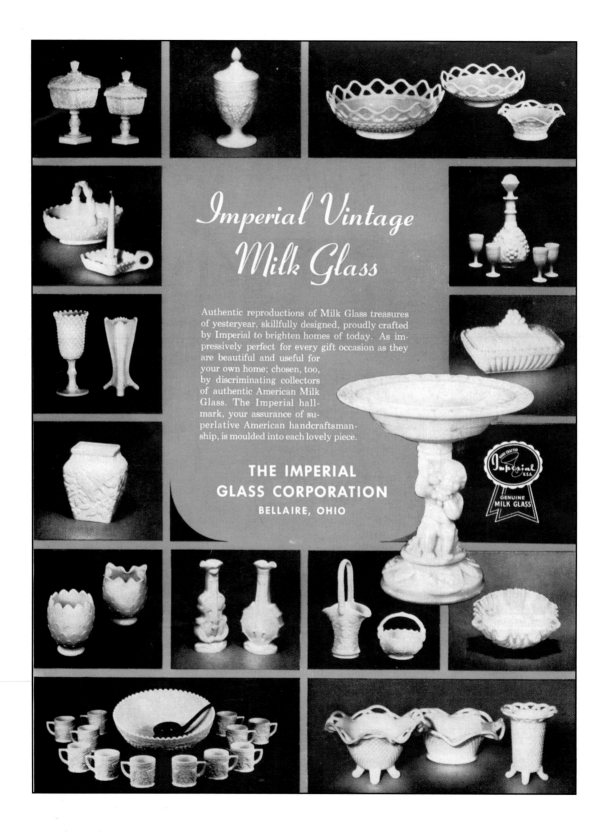

Imperial Vintage Milk Glass

Authentic reproductions of Milk Glass treasures of yesteryear, skillfully designed, proudly crafted by Imperial to brighten homes of today. As impressively perfect for every gift occasion as they are beautiful and useful for your own home; chosen, too, by discriminating collectors of authentic American Milk Glass. The Imperial hallmark, your assurance of superlative American handcraftsmanship, is moulded into each lovely piece.

**THE IMPERIAL
GLASS CORPORATION
BELLAIRE, OHIO**

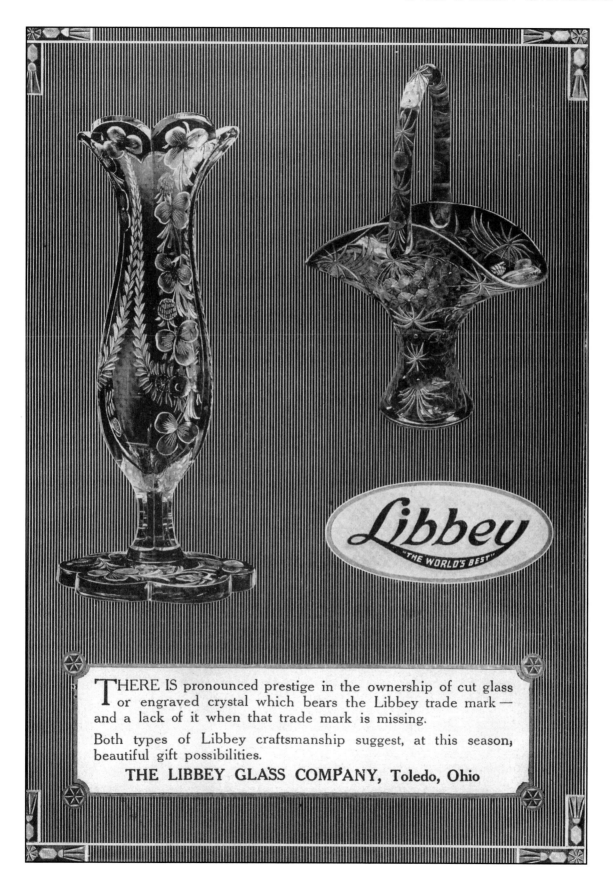

THERE IS pronounced prestige in the ownership of cut glass or engraved crystal which bears the Libbey trade mark — and a lack of it when that trade mark is missing.

Both types of Libbey craftsmanship suggest, at this season, beautiful gift possibilities.

THE LIBBEY GLASS COMPANY, Toledo, Ohio

America's Finest Handmade Milk Glass

Westmoreland's superb, handmade milk glass collection provides a delightful variety of patterns and covers a broad price range. Each piece is readily recognized for its color, fidelity to detail, and hand craftsmanship—qualities that immediately distinguish authentic Westmoreland.

Send 10¢ in coin for Westmoreland Reproduction Booklet

WESTMORELAND GLASS COMPANY
GRAPEVILLE, PENNSYLVANIA

Fine Handmade Glass Since 1889

Fidelity to detail and hand craftsmanship are imperative qualities that have consistently distinguished Westmoreland handmade glassware for sixty-eight years. They are the inherent qualities of Westmoreland handmade glassware today.

Send 10¢ in coin for booklet of Westmoreland Reproductions

WESTMORELAND GLASS COMPANY
GRAPEVILLE, PENNSYLVANIA

Many foods are so appetizing in color . . . it is a shame to hide them in pottery or metal. The pleasing lines and fine transparency of a fluted Viking glass relish dish and platter let you feast doubly—first on color—and then on taste.

(Glass Basket, Candlesticks and Salts also from Viking)

Treasured American Glass from New Martinsville, West Virginia

Viking Glass Company

GAY, GRACEFUL, COLORFUL
Blossom Flite
ARTCRAFT by HULL

For smart centerpieces, for perfect settings for your favorite flowers, for brightening up drab, colorless corners, you'll find just the piece you want in this beautiful artware pattern. Styled in 15 pieces, in your choice of Charcoal-Pink or Blue-Metallic Green color combinations, by HULL POTTERY CO., CROOKSVILLE, OHIO.

OUR 50th YEAR
OF LEADERSHIP

Rosella
for every house beautiful

Hull skilled craftsmen have achieved the dream of fine potters for ages in creating art pottery that justifies its place among your finest possessions. Color baked into the clay, sculptured design tinted under glaze. Ivory or coral. At finer stores throughout the nation.

Free! Ask for ROSELLA folder showing 15 beautiful items. A. E. Hull Pottery Co., Crooksville, Ohio.

HULL
Modern Art Pottery

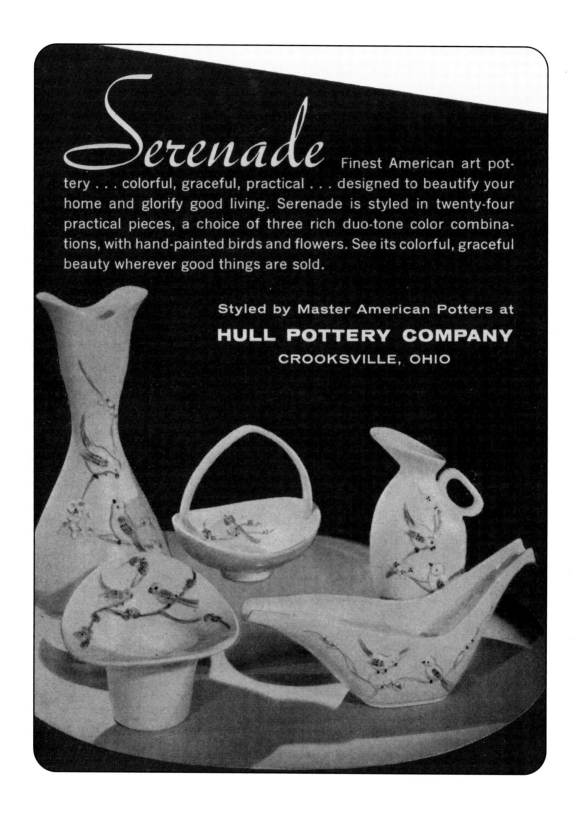

PEONY

DECORATIVE ART POTTERY BY
ROSEVILLE

Beautifully rounded Peony blooms, enhanced by a rich wood-texture finish. 65 graceful new shapes in handpainted Sienna Brown, Coral, Nile Green. At gift shops and department stores.

Send 10c for colorful booklet

ROSEVILLE POTTERY, INC.
Dept. HB-102, Zanesville, Ohio

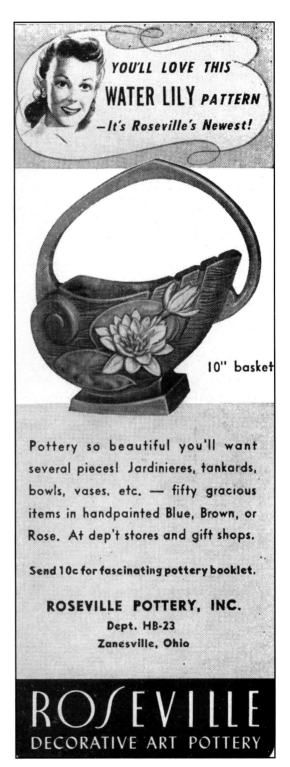

YOU'LL LOVE THIS
WATER LILY PATTERN
—It's Roseville's Newest!

10" basket

Pottery so beautiful you'll want several pieces! Jardinieres, tankards, bowls, vases, etc. — fifty gracious items in handpainted Blue, Brown, or Rose. At dep't stores and gift shops.

Send 10c for fascinating pottery booklet.

ROSEVILLE POTTERY, INC.
Dept. HB-23
Zanesville, Ohio

ROSEVILLE
DECORATIVE ART POTTERY

Bibliography

CAMBRIDGE GLASS

National Cambridge Collectors Inc. *Colors in Cambridge Glass.* Collector Books, Paducah, Kentucky, 1993.

_____. *The Cambridge Glass Co., Cambridge, Ohio.* Collector Books, Paducah, Kentucky, 1976.

Welker, Mary, Lyle, and Lynn. *The Cambridge Glass Co., Cambridge, Ohio, Book 1, A Reprint of Parts of Old Company Catalogues.* Lyle Welker, Concord, Ohio, 1976.

CZECHOSLOVAKIAN & BOHEMIAN GLASS & CERAMICS

Barta, Dale and Diana, and Helen. M. Rose. *Czechoslovakian Glass & Collectibles.* Collector Books, Paducah, Kentucky, 1992.

Forsythe, Ruth. *Made in Czechoslovakia,* Richardson Printing Company, Marietta, Ohio, 1982.

Truitt, Robert and Deborah. *Collectible Bohemian Glass, Vol. II, 1915 – 1945.* B & D Glass, Kensington, Maryland, 1998.

DUGAN/DIAMOND

Burns, Carl O. *Dugan & Diamond Carnival Glass 1909 – 1931.* Collector Books, Paducah, Kentucky, 1999.

Heacock, William, James Measell, and Berry Wiggins. *Dugan/Diamond, The Story of Indiana, Pennsylvania Glass.* Antique Publications, Marietta, Ohio, 1993.

DUNCAN/DUNCAN MILLER

Krause, Gail. *The Encyclopedia of Duncan Glass.* Exposition Press, Hicksville, New York, 1976.

FENTON GLASS

Heacock, William. *Fenton Glass: The First Twenty-Five Years.* O-Val Advertising Corp, Marietta, Ohio, 1978.

_____. *Fenton Glass: The Second Twenty-Five Years.* O-Val Advertising Corp, Marietta, Ohio, 1980.

_____. *Fenton Glass: The Third Twenty-Five Years.* O-Val Advertising Corp, Marietta, Ohio, 1989.

GENERAL GLASS REFERENCE BOOKS

Bredehoft, Tom & Neila. *Fifty Years of Collectible Glass 1920 – 1970.* Antique Trader Books, Iola, Wisconsin, 2000.

Edwards, Bill. *Standard Encyclopedia of Carnival Glass, 5th Edition.* Collector Books, Paducah, Kentucky, 1996.

Florence, Gene. *Elegant Glassware of the Depression Era.* Collector Books, Paducah, Kentucky, 1999.

_____. *The Collector's Encyclopedia of Depression Glass.* Collector Books, Paducah, Kentucky, 1998.

Heacock, William. *Encyclopedia of Victorian Colored Pattern Glass, Book II, Opalescent Glass from A to Z, Second Edition.* Richardson Printing Corp., Marietta, Ohio, 1977.

Madeley, John and Dave Shetlar. *American Iridescent Stretch Glass Identification & Value Guide.* Collector Books, Paducah, Kentucky, 1998.

Miller, Robert W. *The Art Glass Basket.* Wallace-Homestead Book Co., Des Moines, Iowa, 1972.

Newbound, Betty and Bill. *Collector's Encyclopedia of Milk Glass.* Collector Books, Paducah, Kentucky, 1995.

Weatherman, Hazel Marie. *Colored Glassware of the Depression Era 2.* Weatherman Glassbooks, Springfield, Missouri, 1974.

HEISEY GLASS

Bredehoft, Neila. *The Collector's Encyclopedia of Heisey Glass, 1925 – 1938.* Collector Books, Paducah, Kentucky, 1997.

Conder, Lyle, Editor. *Collector's Guide to Heisey's Glassware for Your Table.* L-W Book Sales, Gas City, Indiana, 1984.

IMPERIAL GLASS

Archer, Margaret & Douglas. *Imperial Glass.* Collector Books, Paducah, Kentucky, 1978.

Measell, James, Editor. *Imperial Glass Encyclopedia, Volume I A – Cane.* The Glass Press, Marietta, Ohio, 1995.

_____. *Imperial Glass Encyclopedia, Volume II Cape Cod – L.* The Glass Press, Marietta, Ohio, 1997.

_____. *Imperial Glass Encyclopedia, Volume III M – Z.* The Glass Press, Marietta, Ohio, 1999.

JAPANESE CERAMICS

Spain, David. *Noritake Collectibles A to Z.* Schiffer Publishing, Ltd., Atglen, Pennsylvania, 1997.

Van Patten, Joan F. *The Collector's Encyclopedia of Nippon Porcelain.* Collector Books, Paducah, Kentucky, 1979.

_____. *The Collector's Encyclopedia of Nippon Porcelain, Second Series.* Collector Books, Paducah, Kentucky, 1982.

_____. *The Collector's Encyclopedia of Nippon Porcelain, Third Series.* Collector Books, Paducah, Kentucky, 1986.

_____. *The Collector's Encyclopedia of Noritake.* Collector Books, Paducah, Kentucky, 1984.

_____. *The Collector's Encyclopedia of Noritake, Second Series.* Collector Books, Paducah, Kentucky, 1994.

White, Carole Bess. *Collector's Guide to Made in Japan Ceramics, Book 1.* Collector Books, Paducah, Kentucky, 1996.

_____. *Collector's Guide to Made in Japan Ceramics, Book 2.* Collector Books, Paducah, Kentucky, 1998.

_____. *Collector's Guide to Made in Japan Ceramics, Book 3.* Collector Books, Paducah, Kentucky, 1998.

McKEE GLASS

Stout, Sandra McPhee. *The Complete Book of McKee Glass.* Trojan Press, Inc., North Kansas City, Missouri, 1972.

MORGANTOWN GLASS

Snyder, Jeffrey B. *Morgantown Glass: From Depression Glass Through the 1960s.* Schiffer Publishing, Ltd., Atglen, Pennsylvania, 1998.

NEW MARTINSVILLE GLASS

Measell, James. *New Martinsville Glass, 1900 – 1944.* Antique Publications, Marietta, Ohio, 1994

ROSEVILLE POTTERY

Huxford, Sharon and Bob. *The Collector's Encyclopedia of Roseville Pottery, First Series.* Collector Books, Paducah, Kentucky, 1997.

_____. *The Collector's Encyclopedia of Roseville Pottery, Second Series.* Collector Books, Paducah, Kentucky, 1997.

TIARA

Teal, Ron Sr. *Tiara Exclusives® Company Catalog Reprints.* The Glass Press, Marietta, Ohio, 2000.

TIFFIN/U.S. GLASS

Bickenheuser, Fred. *Tiffin Glassmasters Book I.* Glassmaster Publications, Grove City, Ohio, 1979.

_____. *Tiffin Glassmasters Book II.* Glassmaster Publications, Grove City, Ohio, 1981.

_____. *Tiffin Glassmasters Book III.* Glassmaster Publications, Grove City, Ohio, 1985.

Piña, Leslie and Jerry Gallagher. *Tiffin Glass 1914 – 1940.* Schiffer Publishing, Ltd., Atglen, Pennsylvania, 1996.

WESTMORELAND GLASS

Kovar, Lorraine. *Westmoreland Glass Volume II — 1950 – 1984.* The Glass Press, Inc., Marietta, Ohio, 1991.

_____. *Westmoreland Glass Volume III — 1988 – 1940.* The Glass Press, Inc., Marietta, Ohio, 1997.

Wilson, Chas West. *Westmoreland Glass Identification & Value Guide.* Collector Books, Paducah, Kentucky, 1996.

L.G. WRIGHT GLASS

Measell, James and W.C. "Red" Roettels. *The L.G. Wright Glass Company.* The Glass Press, Marietta, Ohio, 1997.

About the Authors

Carole Bess White is the author of four other books published by Collector Books: *The Collector's Guide to Made in Japan Ceramics, Books 1, 2,* and *3*; and *The Collector's Guide to Lunch Boxes*. She collects and writes in many categories and has been a serious collector of Depression glass since 1971, and a collector of Made in Japan ceramics since 1981.

She is one of the organizers of the annual Portland's Rain of Glass Show and Sale and the American Glass Rally Convention and Seminars presented by Portland's Rain of Glass.

She has been awarded lifetime membership in Portland's Rain of Glass, and is a member of the Noritake Society, the National Cambridge Collectors, the Tiffin Glass Collector's Club, The Paden City Collectors, and the Fostoria Collectors.

Carole has worked full-time in newspaper entertainment advertising for more than 25 years.

L.M. White, Ed.D., has spent many years working with photography and computers. At present he is information technology coordinator for an area K – 12 school. Les is also a lifetime member of Portland's Rain of Glass, even though he collects nothing but computers!

Les and Carole are 1930s and 1940s movie buffs and enjoy decorating their vintage home in Portland, Oregon.